Your First Horse
How to Buy and Care for Your First Horse

Jacqueline Dwelle

Hoofbeat Publications
Southern Pines, North Carolina

Your First Horse
How to Buy and Care for Your First Horse

by Jacqueline Dwelle

Published by:
Hoofbeat Publications
 P. O. Box 2133
Southern Pines, NC 28388-2133 U.S.A.

Library of Congress Cataloging Card Number
Dwelle, Jacqueline
    Your first horse: how to buy and care for your first horse.
    First Edition
    Includes index.
    1. Horses I. Title.
    2. Horsemanship
    SF 285.D9 1997 636.1 - dc20 96-94983
    ISBN 0-9655048-6-7

Dedicated to the memory of
Sandy Minchin

Sandy had a passion for horses, people and life.

About the Author

Jacqueline Dwelle was born in the southern part of England and spent her childhood in the historic New Forest. From an early age she was fascinated with horses and at the age of eight began riding. Her teenage years were spent at horse shows, riding, teaching and caring for horses, ponies and donkeys. As a member of the West Hants Pony Club Jacqueline participated in hunter trials, eventing, dressage, show jumping, mounted games and the pony club tests as far as the "H" level.

After leaving school Jacqueline attended Porlock Vale Equitation Centre where she was immersed in an intensive course leading to the British Horse Society Assistant Instructor certificate (BHSAI).

Now a resident of the United States, Jacqueline has spent the last decade working for top riders and trainers. She has managed barns for J. Michael Plumb and Karen Stives members of the United States Equestrian Team. Currently, she lives in Southern Pines, North Carolina where she works at Pine Meadow Farm, for Ed Minchin. Pine Meadow Farm has produced many notable show horses including The Wizard, Zoom, Texas Tea, Ace in the Hole and Hitech Redneck.

Table of Contents

Warning - Disclaimer

This book is designed to provide information in regard to the subject matter covered. It is sold with the understanding that the publisher and author are not engaged in rendering legal, medical or other professional services. If legal or other expert assistance is required, the services of a competent professional should be sought.

It is not the purpose of this manual to reprint all information that is otherwise available, but to complement, amplify and supplement other texts.

Every effort has been made to make this manual as complete and as accurate as possible. However, there may be mistakes both typographical and in content. Therefore, this text should be used only as a general guide and not as the ultimate source of horse buying/caring information.

The purpose of this manual is to educate and entertain. The author and Hoofbeat Publications shall have neither liability nor responsibility to any person or entity with respect to any loss or damage caused, or alleged to be caused, directly or indirectly by the information contained in this book.

If you do not wish to be bound by the above, you may return this book to the publisher for a full refund.

Acknowledgments

The production of this book has been a learning experience from beginning to end. During the research period, I spent many hours pouring over the notes I had taken whilst a student at Porlock Vale Equitation Center in Somerset, England (unfortunately, no longer in existence.) I also have a large collection of notes inspired by Ann Carter and Mary and John Warden from which a lot of useful information was taken.

Many thanks to all the people who helped with this book, they include: Rick and Ann Thompson, Terry Dennis, Lauren Kuhn, Martin Kenny, Brian and Rita Galloway, Cara Utermehle, Stephen Smith, Susan Barrett, Nancy Hoffman, Jody Scott, Candy Hitchcock and Tim Calcutt. Special thanks to Joan Withey who tirelessly answered all the "What do you think about this?" questions.

To Lenny "I wouldn't have done it without your love and support, thank you."

Cover photograph, kind permission of Joanne Fiedler.

"Don't give your child money. As far as you can afford it, give him horses. No hour of life is lost that is spent in the saddle."

Sir Winston Spencer Churchill

INTRODUCTION

Horses and man have always had close ties. For centuries horses have provided transportation and recreation. They have worked on our farms and carried us in battle. The bond between people and horses is as strong today as it has ever been.

Today's horses continue this long association with man. They can be found in many different situations giving man the unparalleled opportunity to share in a unique partnership. Horse ownership can be extremely rewarding, not only because it provides an opportunity for recreation, but because it offers the chance to form a special friendship with an animal.

This book is written as a tribute to all the special horses I have met in my years in the horse business. Every horse has a character and personality which can be discovered by spending time with him. A lot can be learned about a horse from handling him on the ground. Stable chores may not be as glamorous as riding, however, it is whilst caring for your horse that you really have an opportunity to understand his character.

Horsemanship is not based solely on riding ability. A true horseman is a person who understands the horse's needs and is able to provide for them. A true horseman knows when his horse is hurt or sick and is able to take the correct action to help the animal. A horseman puts his horse before himself and does not ask for more than the horse can give.

Becoming a horseman takes time. Spending time with horses is not sufficient. The time spent must be productive. Knowledge can be learned from books, but practical experience comes with time, practice and patience.

This book is written as a guide for the person who wishes to enhance his life by becoming more closely associated with the horse.

Selecting a horse is quite a daunting task. As well as finding a horse that is suitable for your level and style of riding, you need some assurances that the horse will remain sound and healthy. There is always some speculation involved in buying horses. We can never be one hundred percent certain that the animal in question will not turn out to be a lemon! The chances of making a poor selection can be reduced by acquiring a base of knowledge which directs the decision making process.

Once you have found a horse that suits your needs, providing the best possible care will be your next priority. Caring for your own horse is an incredibly satisfying experience. If time and other commitments require someone else to care for your horse, a knowledge of horse care will give you the satisfaction of knowing that your equine partner is well cared for.

Chapter One

HORSE SHOPPING

Horse ownership is a great responsibility. It requires time, money and commitment. Even if you decide to board your horse and have someone else worry about his day to day care, you are still ultimately responsible for his well being. It is important to select a horse that suits your needs. It is equally important to find a horse which is suited to your level of experience. Finding the right horse requires some work and research, but it is well worth it to have a horse that you can enjoy, respect and with which you can be safe. In this chapter we will discuss how to find the right horse and how to avoid some of the common pitfalls.

DEVELOP AN EQUINE PROFILE

Before you start looking at newspaper ads sit down and list exactly what you want in an equine companion. Many first- time buyers make the mistake of buying the first horse they see because it is pretty or has a famous ancestor. Rarely do these impulse purchases result in good partnerships. There are many factors to be considered when deciding what type of horse you need.

USE

What will the horse be used for? There are five basic categories under this heading.

♦   Pleasure. Trail riding is a very relaxing pastime and often a great social opportunity. Select a horse with comfortable gaits. An agreeable attitude is important, a horse that constantly jigs and fusses soon becomes irritating. A lazy horse will be tiring if you are always reminding him to walk along. Remember that horses may be more forward on a trail than when going around a ring. Select a horse that has been used for trail riding, will cross water, and negotiate other obstacles.

♦   Breeding. The number of first time horse owners buying breeding stock is small. However, you may have plans to breed your favorite mare in the future. If this is the case, select the best you can afford. Avoid any glaring conformation faults.

♦   Working Horses. Although declining in numbers, working horses are still seen especially in the Western states. When purchasing a horse as a working animal, find a horse that knows the job. He can teach you! It will be very hard for two novices to learn a job together. With an experienced horse you will have the peace of mind that the animal will not be frightened by any elements of the job, for example ropes and cattle!

♦   Show Horses. Horse shows are as popular as ever. High prices are commanded for proven winners. This can be big business! Fortunately, there are many small, often unrecognized shows, where anyone can compete on an average horse. Horse shows are a lot of fun and provide goals to work toward. If you wish to seriously compete, prepare to spend a lot of money on equipment, lessons, shipping, and entry fees, not to mention the right horse.

♦ Sport Horses. This category includes horses used for racing, harness races, barrel racing, polo, eventing, show jumping and combined driving. Any horse expected to participate in horse sports needs to be properly conditioned and trained for his sport. For the first time horse owner it is a good idea to purchase a seasoned competitor who knows the ropes and can teach you. Sport horses provide an excellent opportunity to pit your skills against others with similar interests and the competitions are a great way of measuring your progress.

♦ Field Hunters. A good field hunter knows his job. He is comfortable and athletic and has good manners when out hunting. Many breeds of horse are suitable as hunters. Find a horse suited to the terrain you will be hunting over. Horses who have hunted for a couple of seasons are suited to the first-time owner and should provide some good days of sport when properly conditioned.

BREED

Many people have breed favorites and would not be seen dead on a horse of another breed! The breed of the horse is important because some breeds are more suited to certain activities than others. No one breed is perfect for everyone. If you plan to breed your mare at a later date, look for registries that she can be registered with. Part breds often combine the strong points of two breeds. The breed of horse is not as important as its suitability for its intended use. Unless you have specific preferences be flexible in this area or you may overlook a good prospect.

Conformation

Good conformation is desirable in all horses. A well-built horse does not place undue stress on his muscles, tendons and bones, and may therefore stay sounder than a horse with conformation faults. A horse needs to have good conformation for its breed and activity. Of course, there are exceptions to this. The more a horse is expected to do the better his conformation needs to be. On your check list make a note of those conformation faults that your discipline cannot tolerate and those that you could live with if all your other requirements are met.

Age

For the first time horse owner it is strongly recommended that an experienced horse be purchased. A young horse will require training both in the barn and under saddle. Even if you have been taking lessons for several years you are not prepared to train a boisterous youngster all on your own. It would be much better to buy a horse of at least five years of age who has been used for your particular purpose and has been taught some basic barn manners. With good care and correct riding, horses can live into their thirties and often remain useful throughout their twenties.

If you are set on a young horse, consider either buying an older resale project first or a mare to breed. Both these routes will give you the opportunity to gain some practical experience before you take on the challenges of a young horse. There have been many a good young horse ruined by ignorance. NEVER buy a young horse for a novice rider. It is not fair on either the horse or rider. Both will end up scared and possibly hurt.

Temperament and Vices

Some horses are more apt to be nervous and some more docile. A first-time owner does not need a highly strung unpredictable horse. Nor does he need a plug which will only move if he feels so inclined! Somewhere in the middle is ideal. If you are a little timid go for a quieter (not dead) type, which will not be given to spooking and shying.

Regular exercise and a sensible grain ration help to maintain an even disposition. Remember horses, like children, do better with a regular routine. When they feel secure they are quiet, when frightened or scared they will react quickly and nervously.

Vices are any habit which has developed and is undesirable. Determine which vices are not tolerable (rearing, bolting, biting, and kicking - all of these are dangerous) and those which you can cope with (pawing, cribbing, weaving an occasional spook etc.)

SIZE

Size can be a factor in your purchase decision. Buy a horse that is the right size for you! If you are a petite lady go for a small narrower horse. If you are six foot four inches tall, you will need something bigger! It is a simple fact that it is easier to ride a horse that fits you than one that is too large or too small. A big horse will eat more and therefore cost more to keep, do not buy a seventeen hand shire cross unless you actually need a horse of this size! As with anything there are exceptions, but you will look better and feel more comfortable on a horse that fits you.

FASHION

In the horse world there are always fashions. A certain color, breed or cross becomes popular and suddenly there is a glut of these horses. Don't be swayed by fashion! You will not find a suitable partner by looking for what everyone else is riding. Find a horse that suits you, not your best friend!

PRICE

Price is frequently an important aspect of your purchasing decision. Before you start looking, set the maximum amount you will spend and stick to it. Sellers will often try to sell the perfect horse for more than he is worth. Don't be tempted to exceed your limit. Instead make an offer below your limit and negotiate from there.

RESALE VALUE

When you purchase a horse, you are responsible for it until it dies or it is sold. First-time horse owners typically sell their first horse within four years. They either loose interest or they become more interested and more skilled and their equine needs change. Either way, unless you are absolutely sure you will never sell, buy the best you can afford. Horses will appreciate in value if they are winning or their training is improved, otherwise they depreciate. When resale is a possibility, consider buying a registered horse. Remember it costs as much to keep a cheap horse as it does to keep an expensive one.

EQUINE PROFILE

When you have considered all of the above and any other special requirements you may have, you will be armed with a lot of information. The next step is to track down the individual that as closely as possible fills your equine profile. Write down your requirements and take the list with you when you go horse shopping. Certain things will have to be compromised, but the general picture should be fairly clear in your mind and reinforced by the check list. This will save you time in the long run by eliminating horses that are simply not suitable.

WHEN TO BUY

For most of us money is a consideration. To get the best value, try to shop when the prices are at their lowest. The lowest prices are usually in the late fall, because it generally costs more to keep a horse in the winter due to the lack of pasture. Horses may need more bedding and feed in the winter in order to maintain condition and this all adds to the expense. Many people are fair weather riders and lose interest in the winter when riding may not even be possible.

With spring, people's interest is renewed. The laws of supply and demand come into play and consequently horse prices are highest in April, May and June. There is no harm in window shopping during these months, but wait until winter is on the horizon before making an offer.

Do Your Homework

Spend some time studying horses performing in your area of interest. If you are looking for a trail horse, try to find a riding stable that will take you on trail rides or provide lessons. Taking lessons on a horse you are interested in is a great way to try the horse and get to know him a little. Go to shows and other events. Watch the horses that win and the ones that have trouble. If you are planning to take lessons after you buy, there is a chance you might find a horse with some minor problems that your trainer can fix. These horses may be cheaper just because they are not winning.

Don't ignore a horse that is rough looking or has some minor vices. A well-mannered, fat, shiny horse will be more expensive than one which is a little thin, untrimmed and has a pushy nature. Make a careful assessment of your ability to deal with whatever the problems may be. Remember that a quiet horse may become more lively with proper food and care. Not all problems are fixable, it takes a lot of practice to recognize those that are permanent and those that are not.

Ask For Experienced Help

Anyone looking for a horse is strongly advised to seek experienced help. Have a knowledgeable person guide and help you. Even if you do all the research yourself, find someone who knows about the type of horse you are buying to take a look at your final decision, before you write the check! Pay someone if you have to, but get an experienced opinion. There may be some serious fault you have overlooked (and the seller forgot to mention!) that would make the horse unsuitable for you. People qualified to assist in your search for a horse include; your riding instructor, local trainers and veterinarians who specialize horses. Friends who have their own horse are also useful sources to recruit.

Whenever possible spend time with knowledgeable people at shows and other events. Pick their brains and learn as much as you can. Frequently, you can find out about a horse's background by talking to people who have competed against it.

WHERE TO LOOK

Start asking friends and other horse owners about horses in your area that might be for sale. Look in the classified section of the local newspaper. Go to as many horse related events as possible to familiarize yourself with what is available. Visit local stables and farms and talk to the owners. As often as possible have an experienced person accompany you to assist and advise.

When shopping for a specific type of horse, it will be necessary to extend your search area. Subscribe to a state or national magazine. Horses listed in these are usually trained toward a more specific job. To become familiar with the type of horse you are looking for, visit breed shows, events and breeding farms. Be prepared to travel in your search and make some long distance phone calls. Often videos are available of prospects. If you like what you see on tape you can then follow up with a visit.

The more specific your equine profile is, the more you will have to expect to travel. A trail horse can probably be found in your local area but a top class show horse will have to be tracked down.

RESEARCH THE MARKET

The more familiar you are with the market value of horses the less likely you are to pay more than a fair price. This is not always easy especially if you are new to the horse buying industry. Many people make their living buying and selling horses and are knowledgeable about current market values. The first time owner is often willing to pay more than the market value to buy a horse he likes. He is generally not aware of market values and many professional horse traders know this! Again, the advice of an experienced person is essential to determine the market value of a prospect.

Go to auctions and sales to establish the market value of the type of horse you are interested in. This is not a good place to buy, but it is a great place to learn. True market values are apparent from the bidding. There are many draw backs to buying a horse from an auction. There is very little time to assess or try the horse. Vices and lameness may have been temporarily hidden and even scars and blemishes masked. Don't get caught up in the excitement and make an impulse purchase. There are often no guarantees. An express warranty is the closest thing available, for example "warranted sound in wind and limb."

SOURCES

The most common way to buy a horse is through private sale. This allows the buyer time to think through his decision and make calm rational choices. For the first time buyer this is probably the most satisfactory method to use. Most owners are happy for you to visit on more than one occasion and will answer all your questions. If the horse is boarded, be sure to talk to the barn workers to see if they like the horse and if he has any hidden habits!

Breeders are another source of horses. Breeding is an expensive business, and you are likely to pay more for a horse at a breeding farm. If you want a specific breed, this may be the way to go. It is certainly a good way to find out the upper limit of the market.

Breeders and private owners tend to ask more than the market value for their horses. It is also hard to establish a market value for these horses. Advice from an experienced horseman is certainly beneficial at this point.

Another resource to use are agents. These people work for commission, often 15-20% of the purchase price. Many have a listing of available horses and can frequently match up buyers and sellers quickly. Remember, agents are eager for you to buy in order to make their money, so don't be rushed! Think of agents as Realtors for horses. If you are in the market for a specific type of horse this may be a good avenue to try.

No matter where you decide to look for a horse, do not be rushed into anything. Try as many horses as you can and become familiar with the market and market values.

MAKING YOUR DECISION

When you find a prospect which closely fits your equine profile, take your time in assessing the horse. On your first visit to the stable watch closely as the owner handles the horse. Make note of anything you do not like and anything that is especially endearing.

The horse should be able to demonstrate at least some of the things you will expect of him. Watch the owner ride him, and if you like what you see, either ride him your self or have your experienced friend ride him.

Back at the barn ask if you can untack him and cool him out. If they are unwilling for you to do this, be very suspicious. Spend a little time with the horse, pick up his feet and perform other routine tasks. Ask lots of questions. No horse is perfect, try to find out his quirks. There will be some!

If you like what you see, take a look around the stall or pasture. Is the wood chewed excessively? The horse may be a cribber. Observe kick marks on the walls or horse toys in the stall. Notice anything out of the ordinary and ask about it.

There may be a simple explanation or you may have uncovered a potential problem.

After your initial visit, stop by unannounced in order to observe the horse. The owner will not have prepared him and you may catch something you missed on the first trip. Ask to take a lesson on the horse. Tack up the horse yourself and spend as much time as possible around him. The more time you spend with a horse the more likely you are to detect any unwanted habits.

TRIAL PERIOD

During a trial period, you have an opportunity to assess the horse in its new surroundings. This is a great way to confirm that you are making the right decision. A trial period is usually one or two weeks. Have an agreement in writing stating the length of time the horse is to be tried before any money changes hands. The condition of the horse when it left the seller should also be included. You also need to have a written agreement as to who is responsible for any unforeseen expenses during the trial period, in case of colic, accidents and other unexpected events.

PRE PURCHASE EXAM

This is strongly recommended for every potential purchase. A pre-purchase exam is not a guarantee from the Vet, but it will often reveal minor problems that may cause a loss in performance. Following a pre-purchase the Vet should be able to state that in his opinion the horse is either physically suited or not suited for his intended purpose. This is all you can expect from a pre-purchase exam, however, it is worth knowing exactly what you will be dealing with and in some instances avoid making an expensive mistake.

Since the Vet is working for the buyer, he should not be the horse's regular Vet. Only have the horse vetted when you have decided that this is the horse you want. If you take the horse on trial, have him vetted towards the end of the trial period. A vet check can be customized to meet your needs. A pleasure horse will require a less stringent test than a horse to be used for competition or resale.

Most Vets follow a similar pattern. The Vet will look at the teeth and age the horse. Older horses are harder to age than young ones, but he should be able to get an indication within a year. This is important for all horses. The Vet should question the seller as to any past health problems, for example systemic diseases and serious injuries and if possible get a signed statement from the seller stating that the horse has no known history of health problems.

Deworming and vaccination records should be discussed. These will need to be obtained if you purchase the horse in order to continue with them at the correct intervals.

A physical exam should be conducted. The purpose of this is to detect any abnormalities. During a physical exam the Vet will go over the horse from head to toe, take the horse's temperature, listen to the heart and lungs, and examine the eyes. The conditions which may be found include: teeth problems, damage to one or both eyes, heaves, abnormal heart sounds, a history of founder, one side more developed than the other and indications of behavioral or training problems. He can assess each problem and advise you on the probable affect upon the horse.

The physical exam is followed by a lameness assessment. This will further investigate any abnormalities and may reveal hidden soundness problems.

The Vet will examine the feet with hoof testers looking for navicular disease, contracted heels, thin or bruised soles and other potential problems. He will watch the horse trot from the front and rear. Flexion tests will be conducted to detect problems in the joints. The horse will be lunged or ridden at the walk, trot and canter in both directions to reveal any unsoundness. The Vet will listen to the breathing to detect any noises when the horse is working.

Radiographs are usually taken at the request of the buyer. They can reveal changes in the feet and joints. Whether to take X-rays depends on the purpose for which the horse will be used and the amount of money being spent. If a problem shows up radiographs can give a better picture of the seriousness. Any horse being bought for resale needs a set of X-rays. When you are ready to sell these can be a great asset. Current X-rays can be compared with older ones to demonstrate how quickly the feet and joints are changing.

If none is available, blood for a coggins test should be taken and for an extremely valuable horse drug tests can be conducted. Another consideration is a fecal exam to indicate the past standards of care. Blood can also be drawn to test for anemia and other disorders.

It is up to the buyer to decide how thorough the vet check will be. The more money you are spending on the horse the more thorough the vetting should be.

When the vetting is done and all the tests and radiographs are back from the lab, the Vet will give his opinion as to the suitability of the horse for its intended purpose. Frequently, small problems are found. Listen to what he has to say and then make your final decision.

EQUINE PROFILE

What will the horse be used for?

Is resale a consideration?

Do you have a preference as to whether you buy a mare or a gelding?

Breed preferences.

Do you want a registered horse?

Conformation. What can you live with?

Age range.

Temperament.

Vices you can tolerate.

Size range.

Horses level of training.

Maximum price.

Other considerations.

Chapter Two

CONFORMATION

When looking for a horse it is helpful to have an understanding of conformation, i.e. form as it relates to function. This can be very confusing for first time horse owners, so spending as much time as possible around horses and horse people will help develop an appreciation of quality. This is an area which is initially overwhelming but becomes easier with practice. Don't forget you can always ask your knowledgeable friend to confirm your conclusions.

Conformation is simply the study of the way a horse is built as it relates to the way the horse moves and performs. A well-built horse will be more athletic than one with a glaring fault or defect. A straight-legged horse will move straight, a crooked legged horse will move crookedly.

Conformation is important to evaluate a horse's probable future soundness. A well built horse is more likely to stay sound than one which has conformational weaknesses. Good conformation is not a guarantee of future soundness, but it is a place to start when evaluating a horse's usefulness and durability.

Horses are athletes and soundness is essential to their usefulness. This is why it is important to have a knowledge of basic conformation before you go shopping for a horse. If you already own a horse, evaluating his strengths and weaknesses will help you understand why he is good at some things and not so good at others.

Good conformation is often accompanied with good movement. Good movement places a minimal amount of stress on the horse. A good mover is more likely to stay sound than a poor mover.

How To Assess Conformation

Horses are large animals with many components. Initially evaluating a horse's build seems like a massive task. To make the evaluation understandable and logical, break it up into several sections and use a system to judge each horse you see. Once you are familiar with the system it becomes easier to judge each horse and make a reasonable evaluation of its merits.

The discussion that follows applies to the mature horse. Young horses go through many stages in their development, and some of the guidelines below will not necessarily apply to a horse that is still growing. (Horses can continue to grow until five or six years old, after three years of age the adult conformation will be apparent. As the animal grows it is common for the hindquarters to grow faster than the forehand giving the appearance of being higher behind. At maturity the forehand will be the same height as the hindquarters.) Assessing a young horse requires a lot of experience and practice and should be left to someone with many years of experience in this area.

Overview

Stand back and look at the whole horse. Is the whole picture pleasing to the eye or does something stand out right away? In the initial evaluation consider these four basic qualities balance, smoothness, substance and definition. These four qualities are the guidelines that are used to assess the horse as a whole, and later to assess the many parts that make up the whole.

BALANCE

The forehand should be roughly the same size as the hindquarters. The appearance is one of harmony and equilibrium. The legs are approximately the right length for the body, and the head is neither too small or too large. When all is balanced, the horse has a well proportioned look about him.

SMOOTHNESS

All the major areas-the head and neck, the forehand, the body and the hindquarters-should be attached to one another without any abrupt angles. Just like a sports car the horse has smooth lines!

SUBSTANCE

Substance refers to quality combined with sturdiness and to strength without coarseness. Refinement with good definition is desirable, especially for the head and legs. Substance is often used to describe the chiseled, proportionate appearance of the head and legs, but in your initial evaluation look at the whole horse for substance.

DEFINITION

Ideally, the horse should have the features of a body-builder! His muscles should be well developed showing a clear outline of the flesh below the skin. Where the bones are close to the surface these too should be smooth and free from bumps. Fleshiness and loose skin indicate coarseness about the horse. Remember a horse that is unfit and at grass will have less definition than a fit stabled horse. Find out how fit the horse is before starting your evaluation.

Consider each of the above factors as you view the horse as a whole. Look at the head and neck and progress to the body and legs. Look at the way the legs attach to the body, they should give the appearance of a leg in each corner. The legs should be straight when viewed from the front, back and both sides. Your first overall impression should be one of smoothness and balance. A well-defined horse with plenty of substance.

The next step is to break the horse up into its parts and assess each part for its strengths and weaknesses.

THE TOP LINE

The top line runs from behind the ears down the neck to the withers, along the back to the top of the tail. Apply balance, smoothness, substance and definition to this line. Each part should run smoothly into the next, no one area being proportionally larger than another. A strong top line sets a horse off and is an indication of strength. In a mature horse the hindquarters and the forehand should be the same height.

THE NECK

The neck needs to fit the head and the body. A well built neck is muscled from the poll to the withers. The most common faults of the neck are ewe neck, where the muscles in front of the withers are not well developed, and an overly cresty neck which will make bending difficult.

THE WITHERS

Well pronounced withers that taper gently into the back will provide a good place for the saddle to sit. Flat withers and a neck that is set on low will make flexion and bending difficult. Withers which are very large can be injured, and make saddle fitting difficult.

THE BACK

Short backs are stronger than long backs. Measure the coupling (the space between the last rib and the point of hip) with your fist. If the space is wider than one fist, the horse is said to be "short of a rib." A long backed horse will have trouble stepping under himself; a short backed horse may not be as supple as you would like. Well-sprung ribs that blend into the shoulders and hips usually accompany shorter backs.

THE HINDQUARTERS

The hindquarters provide the power and balance needed for any kind of work. Good muscular development is desirable for the horse's engine. Flat quarters with a high set tail reduce the horse's ability to step under himself. A low set tail increases the length of spine therefore creating possible weakness. Horses with low set tails appear to be crouching.

THE BOTTOM LINE

Running from the throat, between the front legs along the belly to the sheath, the bottom line is equally as important as the top line. The windpipe needs to be well defined and wide enough for good breathing. An excessive amount of muscle on the lower neck may indicate a horse with a high, stiff head carriage or possibly a cribber.

THE CHEST

The chest should have plenty of room for the heart and lungs. Width is important when viewed from the front. A very narrow chest may cause the horse to knock himself with the opposite leg (interfering). A chest that looks like a bull dog's (excessively wide) may cause the forelegs to swing out as the horse moves (dishing or paddling).

THE GIRTH

The girth needs to be deep to provide plenty of room for the heart and lungs. As a rough guide measure the girth all around. It should be approximately equal to the height from the withers to the floor.

THE BELLY

The shape of the belly will depend upon the state of fitness, although, the general outline should taper away to the sheath. The greyhound look is not desirable!

THE HEAD

Many first time horse owners fall in love with a horse's head and forget the rest of the animal. Avoid this temptation as it will lead you into trouble later.

The head should fit the body. Apply the four principals (balance, smoothness, substance and definition) to the head. A quality horse will have a chiseled head with the skin stretched tightly across the bones. The head should be either feminine or masculine depending on the sex of the horse.

The eyes should be large, clear and friendly. Small piggy eyes are often associated with a mean or bad tempered horse. The area between the eyes should be wide and flat creating a good forehead.

The ears should have a good space between them and be carried in an alert fashion. A horse who constantly flicks his ears back and forth is probably nervous. One who pins them often may have a mean streak. Watch the horse's expression as he is groomed or tacked up it will tell you a lot about the horse's disposition.

If you plan to use the horse for fast work the size of the nostrils is important. They should have the capacity to expand enabling a large intake of air when needed. To test this, place your fingers in the nostril and see how much expansion is available. Another test of the airways is to place your fist between the cheek bones. You should be able to fit your fist comfortably between the cheekbones of any potential performance horse.

A horse with a small mouth may have trouble with the bit, as there will not be much room to fit the bit without touching the teeth.

Look at the thickness of the throat. A horse that is thick through the throat will have trouble flexing at the pole. Look for refinement and definition in any horse that needs to carry his head in a flexed position.

THE BODY

The body needs to suit the rest of the animal. A draft horse will require a heavier body than a race horse. During the discussions of the top and bottom lines we talked about the overall appearance of the body. In this section we are going to take a look at the build of the body and how it relates to movement and hence future soundness. A horse that continually puts excess pressure on his legs is more likely to develop soundness problems.

The body is divided into the forehand, the back and the hindquarters. In a horse that moves well the bones in the shoulder and the hindquarters are long, causing the angles that they form to be acute. This causes three things to happen.

1.   There is less direct downward stress on the limbs, therefore less wear and tear.

2.   The withers are set well back, relieving the rider of the direct jarring of the forelegs.

3.   The joints are better able to straighten, increasing the combined length of the bones and therefore the length of the horse's stride.

THE FOREHAND

Obviously, the forehand dictates how the forelegs move. The length and angles in the shoulder will give a good idea of how long a stride the horse will be capable of taking and whether his action will be smooth or choppy.

Look at the shoulder. Ideally, the shoulder slopes at 45° from the vertical. Compare the length of the shoulder to the length of the head. The shoulder should be at least as long as the head.

Draw an imaginary line from the center of the withers through the point of shoulder and extend it to the ground. This should be close to 45°. Where this line hits the ground is approximately where the horse will be able to place his

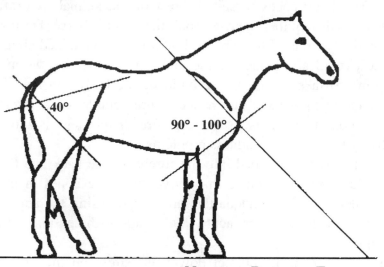

MAXIMUM POINT OF EXTENSION

foot at maximum extension, or his maximum length of stride.

Draw a second line from the point of shoulder to the elbow. Where this line bisects the shoulder line we have the angle of the shoulder. Ideally this angle is 90° - 100°.

Compare the shoulder slope to the slope of the pasterns. Because angles repeat throughout the body, the pasterns should have the same slope as the shoulder. A long sloping shoulder is usually accompanied by a long sloping pastern. Pasterns of a good length and angle are desirable as they act as shock absorbers. Short upright pasterns will produce a short choppy stride. Going to the other extreme, an excessively long pastern will place extra strain on the tendons and produce a slow swinging stride.

Combine good shoulder and pastern length with the correct angles, and you have a horse that moves with good extension and plenty of freedom. Any deviation from these guidelines will probably indicate a horse with less than perfect action.

THE HINDQUARTERS

The hindquarters provide the power needed to move and balance the horse. They are the horse's engine and therefore need to be well muscled. How far a horse can step underneath himself will dictate the length of stride and how much power he is capable of producing.

The hip joint is an important angle because it will give you a clue as to how much length of stride to expect. As the hindquarters carry more muscle than the shoulder it is hard to accurately imagine the angles. (Do the best you can, this is not a test!) With practice you will get a feel for what is right and what is not. To find the hip joint angle, draw an imaginary line from the point of hip through the hip joint (this is located directly in front of the point of buttock). Draw the second line from the hip joint to the stifle. These lines will lie where the bones are located underneath. Look at the angle. An ideal hip joint angle is 40°, which would give a good deep step that will effortlessly propel the horse forward.

Assess the croup. For a good length of stride the croup should be long and reasonably level. This area is a power house and therefore needs to be well developed. Short and steep croups are usually accompanied by short strides causing a horse to place extra stress on the front legs by being on his forehand (dragging his body with the front legs instead of pushing himself with his hindquarters.)

Leverage is important when producing power. For maximum leverage the hips and the hocks need to be well apart. This will place the hocks close to the ground creating short cannon bones. Short cannon bones are a desirable feature because there are no muscles below the knee or hock. Any movement is caused by muscles higher up in the body and a system of tendons and ligaments. The shorter the cannon bones, the less the chance of an injured tendon or ligament.

Another way to test the hindquarters is to lift the tail and observe the long muscles running down the back of the hind legs to the gaskins. These muscles should be well developed and well defined. If they are weak the horse may take short, weak steps when he moves.

THE LEGS AND FEET

The horse's primary function is to be an athlete. To fulfill this roll he must possess strong, well-built legs that move with the minimum amount of stress to themselves. Pay particular attention to the legs and feet when assessing conformation as they are vital to the horse's usefulness.

During your overview of the horse, any glaring faults should have been noticed and the general development of the

Normal	Back at the Knee and Tied-in-Below the Knee	Over at the Knee

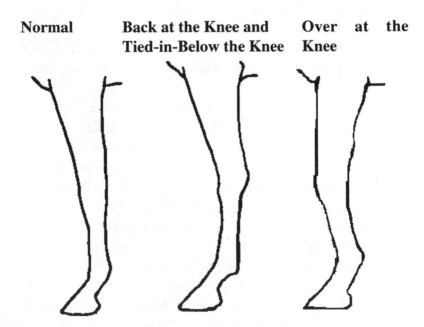

legs and feet observed. It is now time to take a closer look at the legs and feet. As you do this try to relate any faults to future soundness and evaluate how a particular flaw will affect performance.

Straightness is of utmost importance to the legs. A horse with straight legs will probably move straight. Think of the parts of the leg as a set of blocks sitting on top of each other. If one block is slightly out of line, it will place more pressure on the blocks below it.

THE FORELEGS

Stand at the side of the horse and draw a line from the center of the shoulder to the ground. When the horse is standing squarely, this line will split the leg into two halves all the way to the fetlock joint. From the fetlock it will drop behind the pastern and finish at the back of the heel. If the two halves are not equal, there is a possibility that over time the stress will take its toll on the legs and cause lameness.

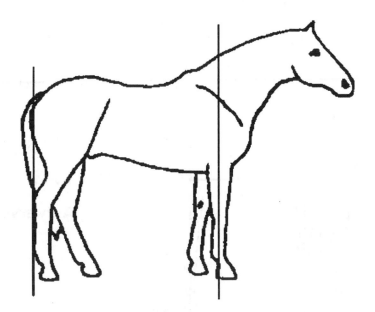

Assess the degree of deviation. A minor deviation will cause less trouble than a major one.

Step around to the front of the horse. Drop a line from the point of the shoulder to the ground. This line should bisect the leg perfectly. The knees should appear large and flat. The cannon bone, fetlock and foot should be equal on each side of this line.

As you assess the degree of straightness compare the two forelegs with one another. They should be identical. The feet should be of the same size and their angle should be the same as the angle of the pastern (45°). Generally, the larger the feet the better. The joints should be large and free of puffiness. Substance and definition are important in the joints of the leg. Look at the cannon and splint bones for splints on both the inside and outside of the leg. Run your hand over any suspicious lumps, feeling for heat, pain and swelling.

Notice how the legs are attached to the body. There should be room between the elbow and the body for a fist. From the front, the legs should appear as two parallel lines. If they form a "V" in any way there is weakness.

THE HIND LEGS

The imaginary vertical line for the hind leg starts at the point of buttock. It should touch the point of the hock and

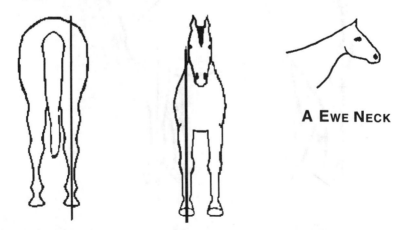

A EWE NECK

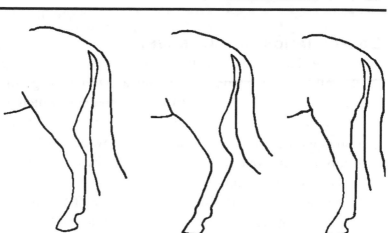

GOOD HOCK ANGLE,   SICKLE HOCKS,   STRAIGHT HOCKS

run down the back of the cannon bone (or a hair behind it) to the ground. There should be plenty of muscular development on the thighs and gaskin. The hocks are naturally a rather knobby joint. They need to be large, flat and free of swelling or puffiness. Gently feel for swelling, especially on the front of the hock.

The cannon bones of the hind legs are naturally a little longer than the ones of the forelegs. Again look for splints, and other signs of weakness and compare the feet. The angle of the pastern and foot is 55° for the hind leg.

Move round behind the horse and carefully move the tail to one side. Drop two imaginary vertical lines from the point of buttock to the ground. Each line should bisect the hock, the ergot and the center of the foot. The two halves of the leg should be equal and the two lines parallel. Many horses are to some extent cow-hocked. This means that the legs are built so that the toes turn out and the point of hocks turn in towards one another. In moderation this is not a serious weakness.

CONFORMATION AND MOVEMENT

A horse that moves well takes large steps. The forelegs reach well forward in front of the body and touch the ground gently. The movement comes from the shoulders which are free to provide maximum extension or length of stride. The hindquarters are powerfully built. At the walk and trot the hind foot falls in front of the hoof print left by the front foot. This is called over tracking.

Good movement is desirable in any horse. The basics of good movement are the same for all disciplines and styles of riding. Specific breeds may have their own special requirements, however, the basics that are discussed in this section can be applied to horses in general. A good mover is balanced, straight and smooth.

Balance is seen when the horse shifts his weight onto his hindquarters as he moves and propels himself forward from behind. This frees the shoulders allowing them to move freely therefore reaching maximum extension. A horse that carries too much weight on his forehand will drag his hind legs behind him. His shoulders will be working to drag him along and will not be able to produce a good length of stride.

Straight movement occurs when the hind legs exactly follow the path of the front legs. Each foot swings forward from the ground and travels in a straight line under the body until it touches down again.

A smooth gaited horse wastes no energy in his steps. The feet touch the ground lightly and evenly. This reduces concussion and minimizes the wear and tear on the legs and feet.

FAULTS IN MOVEMENT

When movement deviates from the straight, smooth, balanced action described above, the legs may suffer. Over time this faulty action may cause excessive wear and tear on the joints causing lameness problems to occur.

PADDLING OR DISHING

A horse with pigeon toes will swing his forelegs to the outside as he moves them forward. He appears to be paddling. The paddling occurs from the knee down. This is energy wasted and the horse will tire easily.

WINGING OR PLAITING

Winging is usually seen with a horse whose toes turn out (splayed feet.) As the foot travels forward it swings inwards. In extreme cases the foot may land directly in front of its partner. This is called plaiting. The problem with this type of movement is that the horse is likely to hit the opposite leg with his hoof, causing injury. An example of interfering.

COMMON CONFORMATION FAULTS

Deviations from the ideal are very common. Often they appear as a group of related flaws. A horse with one or two minor deviations is preferred over one with a series of flaws. The table which follows indicates which faults can be tolerated. Conformation faults can be lived with if the horse is being purchased for light or slow work. Horses intended for the show ring, racing or other demanding sports should be as correct as possible.

CONCLUSION

When assessing a horse look at the over all picture first. Use the table as a guide, and with practice, obvious faults will leap out at you as will good points. Don't be put off by minor faults but assess them with future performance in mind. Can you live with these problems? Will they reduce the horse's useful life? If resale is a possibility then these imperfections must be assessed with this in mind. When assessing each area of the horse look for defects and strong points. Weigh up the degree of the problem and look for other related problems. Ask a lot of questions relating to any defects that you find. Inquire about the past soundness of the horse.

If at all possible have your experienced friend evaluate the horse with you. Two heads are better than one! When the horse is vetted, ask the Vet to assess his conformation and point out any defects, explain them and summarize their potential problems. You are paying the Vet for his expertise so it is a smart move to mine this resource. Listen to what he has to say and then make your own decisions based upon the available information.

POINTS OF THE HORSE

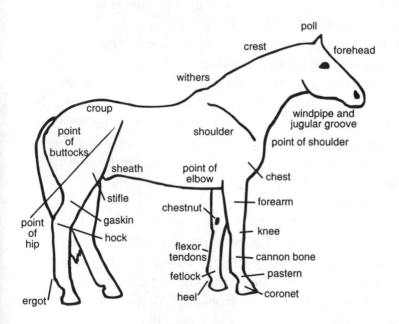

Fault	Appearance	Potential Problems	Severity
Back at the knee or calf-kneed	Side View. Knee appears pushed back behind the rest of the leg. The leg appears concave.	Places strain on the check ligament and the knee joint. Most of the leg will fall behind the ideal vertical line.	Acceptable in horses intended for light or slow work.
Barrel-chested	Overly rounded rib cage. Appears top heavy.	Often accompanied by little heart room. Saddle fitting a problem.	Common in quarter horses. OK for slow work.
Base-narrow	The feet are closer than the shoulders or buttocks. "V" formed by imaginary lines.	Exerts strain on the outside of the feet and legs. Ringbone, sidebone and outside splints. Horse may knock himself as he moves.	OK if horse does not interfere
Base-wide	Opposite of base-narrow. Legs form upside-down "V".	Inside stress. Ringbone, sidebone and inside splints	OK if horse does not interfere
Bench knees	When viewed from the front, the cannon bone does not sit directly below the knee. It is to the outside of the knee.	Uneven stress on cannon bone. Splints and possible arthritis in the knee.	OK in mild forms
Bow legs	Knees or hocks curve out.	Stresses joints and suspensory mechanisms	Best Avoided

Fault	Appearance	Potential Problems	Severity
Camped-out	Either one or both sets of legs stand outside the ideal vertical line.	Caused by over straight pasterns. In front may indicate disease. Behind, indicates a problem with using the haunches.	
Camped-under	Hind legs in front of the ideal vertical line.	Stress the hocks and ligaments.	A bad fault.
Coon-footed	A long pastern with a greater slope than the hoof.	Causes excessive stress on the tendons and ligaments at the back of the leg.	A bad fault.
Cow-hocked	Hocks turn towards one another.	If slight it is not a problem. When severe may cause spavin or interfering.	Very common. Not serious unless severe. Common in arabians.
Croup-high	Croup is higher than the withers.	Requires extra effort to provide sufficient power and forward push.	OK if not too severe.
Knocked-kneed	When viewed from the front the knees point at one another.	Places stress on the joints and tendons.	A bad fault.
Light in the pants	Rear view of the hind legs. Muscles are weak and under developed.	May shuffle along or move wide behind. May lack push from behind.	OK for a pleasure horse. Can be improved with hill work.

Fault	Appearance	Potential Problems	Severity
Mule-footed	The hoof is small and boxy with narrow heels.	Little feet absorb less shock and are prone to navicular.	A bad fault.
Over at the knee or buck-kneed	Leg appears convex. Knee is pushed forward in front of the rest of the leg.	Considered to be less serious than back at the knee. May cause side bones.	A bad fault.
Pigeon-toed or toeing in	Toes point towards each other	May cause the horse to paddle. Stresses inside of leg, causing inside splints.	OK for light or slow work.
Post legs	Excessively straight hind legs. Most of the hock is in front of the imaginary vertical line.	Stresses the stifle joint and can lead to spavins.	OK for light work.
Sickle-hocked	Excessive angle to the hock. Bringing foot too far under body.	Places stress on the hocks. Causes spavins and curbs.	OK for pleasure horse.
Slab-sided	Barrel lacks substance. The horse has poor "rib spring".	Little heart/lung room. Saddle fitting may be a problem.	OK. Horse may not be a comfortable ride.
Splayed-feet or toeing out	Feet turn out often from the knee or hock.	Causes winging and dishing when moving.	OK for light work.
Stand under in front	Horse looks like he is leaning into the wind.	Increases strain on front feet, and causes excessive wear on ligaments and tendons.	OK if not severe.

Fault	Appearance	Potential Problems	Severity
Tied in below the knee	Tendons at the back of the cannon bone are pulled in tight to the knee. The leg appears pinched behind the knee.	Shows weakness in the tendons and ligaments. May not stand up to a lot of pounding.	OK for light work.
Tied-in elbow	Elbow joint is snugly attached to the body.	Restricts the length of stride. Horse may shuffle.	OK if not severe.
Upright pasterns	Pastern is closer to the vertical than is desirable.	Concussion through-out the foot is increased. Continual pounding can lead to ringbone or sidebone.	Best avoided. Horse will be uncomfortable to ride. Common in quarter horses.
Wide-forked	Front legs appear far apart.	Horse may wing or plait as he moves	OK unless horse inter-feres.

Chapter Three

FEEDING

Feeding the horse is not a mystery. It requires a knowledge of feed products, different hays, grasses and supplements. Following a set of feeding guidelines will help you to understand the horse's nutritional needs. When planning a feeding program it is important to be aware of the types of feed stuffs available in your area. The quality of grass may vary from place to place depending upon the climate and farming practices in the area. A good place to start when planning what to feed is the pasture. Does the horse receive any nutritional value from the time he spends in the paddock? Is his turn-out time strictly for exercise? Or does he live in a large lush pasture?

Having evaluated how much (if any) nutrition the horse receives from grass consider how much work the horse will be expected to do. Is he simply 'yard-art' or is he expected to take you on long trail rides? What is his function?

FEEDING GUIDELINES

The following feeding guidelines should always be in the back of your mind. They are tested principals which will help ensure the good health of your horse.

Feed little and often.	This emulates the horse's natural dining habits as closely as possible.
Keep feed buckets clean.	This is important because the smell of stale or moldy feed can discourage a horse, who is at all picky, from eating.
Feed plenty of bulk food like hay or grass	Again, this as closely as possible mimics the horses natural dining habits. Naturally horses are grazers and in a wild state will graze for most of the day. Their stomachs are used to a steady supply of fibrous food. This fiber is essential for correct digestion.
Plan a feeding program around the horses age, temperament and work	If you plan to put your horse on a fitness program you will need to adjust his feed as his work increases. If he is laid up for a time his feed must be cut back. Young horses require food in order to develop correctly. Old horses often have higher nutritional needs because of failing teeth and digestive upsets. A highly strung horse may benefit from eating more bulk (hay and grass) and less energy creating foods (grain.) Conversely a quiet lazy character can benefit from some extra energy!
Make no sudden changes in diet or feeding routine.	As mentioned earlier horses are creatures of habit and any disturbance in their routine can upset them and in turn be detrimental to good health. Changes often need to be made in routines and diet. Just remember to make these changes over a day or two to make the adjustment as easy as possible.

Feed good quality feed.	Especially, be aware of dusty or moldy hay which can cause coughs and colic. Always inspect new hay and feed for mold and return it to your dealer if you do not like what you see. Feed merchants are usually willing to work with you because their reputation is on the line!
Never feed a hot horse.	Always be sure to cool your horse down after work. Feeding a hot horse will prevent correct cooling and can lead to colic.
Wait at least one hour after feeding to exercise the horse.	After a meal the blood supply is concentrated on the digestive process. If you ask the horse to work immediately after eating he will be unable to digest his food properly and the result may be colic.
Provide plenty of fresh clean water	Water should be available at all times. It is needed for digestion cooling and many other bodily processes. Scrub buckets and troughs every day and refill with fresh water

NUTRITIONAL NEEDS

It is important to understand the composition of feed products and how they relate to your horse's needs. The main components of a diet, be it equine or human, are:

◆   Carbohydrates: Produce energy and heat. Extra is converted to fat and stored under the skin.

◆   Proteins: Muscle and tissue building.

◆   Fat: The horse's digestive system can only cope with small amounts of fat. The little that is absorbed is stored as body fat.

◆   Fiber: Is essential for digestion and to keep the digestive muscles toned up. Especially important in the equine diet. The major source of fiber is hay and grass.

♦   Minerals: Build and maintain the skeleton. Used in cell production and other bodily processes.

♦   Vitamins: Found in feed stuffs, needed for main bodily functions.

Generally the horse's diet should consist of at least 50% fiber, 30% carbohydrates, 10% protein and 10% fat.

How much to feed

When deciding how much to feed, take into consideration the type of horse. Is he lazy, average or high strung? Does he carry his weight well or is it hard to keep the pounds on him? Also consider his height and build, the work he will be doing, his age and the environment in which he lives. In cold climates horses will require more bulk in their diet to keep warm. Always remember horses are individuals, some will require more food and some less.

The best way to decide how much to feed is to start feeding your horse according to these guidelines, and as time goes by adjust the rations to compensate for changes in body weight, energy levels, the time of the year, workload and fitness level.

The table is meant as a rough guide for an average type of horse, doing one hour of light work, five times a week. Divide these quantities into two or three feeds per a day.

Size	Average Body Weight	Amount of food per day	Hay or Grass versus Concentrates
13h.h.	500 lbs.	14 lbs.	12 lbs. hay, 2 lbs. grain
14h.h.	700 lbs.	18 lbs.	14 lbs. hay, 4 lbs. grain
15h.h.	900 lbs.	25 lbs.	20 lbs. hay, 5 lbs. grain
16h.h.	1000 lbs.	28 lbs.	22 lbs. hay, 6 lbs. grain
17h.h.	1200 lbs.	30 lbs.	22 lbs. hay, 8 lbs. grain

A horse will consume 1.5% to 2% of its body weight a day. For an idle horse this can be all in the form of roughage - grass and hay.

Another way of estimating how much to feed is to take the horse's height subtract two and multiply by two, for example:

$$(16 \text{ hands} - 2) \times 2 = 28$$

This formula works for horses over fifteen hands. Ponies often require a lot less food than these equations suggest. As work is increased more grain and concentrates will be needed and less roughage will be consumed. The roughage content of the diet should never drop below a third of the total intake because roughage is vital for digestion and maintaining the digestive tract.

There are weight tapes available which when used to measure the horse's girth will estimate the horse's weight.

DECIDING WHAT TO BUY

As mentioned in the feeding guidelines, buy the best quality forage for your horse. Hard feed comes in several different forms, with each offering different levels of nutrition and digestibility. By choosing. the right type of hay for your horse and complementing this with the correct form of hard feed, it is possible to provide a well balanced diet at an affordable price.

HAY

Good hay is one of the most important purchases you can make for your horse. Good quality hay provides not only fiber in the equine diet, but also an anti-boredom tool for horses that spend many hours standing in a stall or pen. For the horse owner it is worth the investment to buy good quality hay. There will be little waste, the horse will be content, and part or all of his nutritional needs will be met. For a horse in light work it is possible to feed hay and a very small amount or no grain. There are two ways of producing hay: seed hay and meadow hay. Seed hay is grown as a rotation crop and tends to be higher in protein. Meadow hay is cut from permanent pasture and is softer to the touch, it is more easily digested.

SPOTTING QUALITY HAY

Good quality hay can come from any part of the country. Weather conditions play an important roll in the production and therefore the price of hay. The main areas that produce hay are the North East and the Mid West. Open a bale and look at the hay inside. Here is what to look for:

♦   A good color. A bright green color is desirable as this is correlated to the carotene content. Some perfectly good hay may be light brown due to sun bleaching. Avoid dark brown hay, this has probably suffered heat damage and yellow hay has been exposed to the weather for too long. The bale should not be hot inside; overheated hay does not make good horse feed.

♦   Composition. What grasses make up the hay? What percentage of each type of grass is present?

♦   Aroma. The hay should not smell musty or moldy. It should be sweet smelling and not dusty.

♦   Foreign objects. Don't buy hays that contain a lot of weeds or foreign seed heads such as burrs and thorns. Also avoid hay with trash of other unwanted material that is visible. Occasionally hay will contain an odd piece of trash but this should be the exception not the rule.

♦   Leafiness. The nutritional value of the hay is in the leaves. Look for hay with a good proportion of leaves and few coarse stems.

♦   Maturity. The best hay is harvested when the seed heads are just beginning to form. For legumes there should be no more than a quarter of the hay with seed heads and for grass hays the hay should be cut when the seed heads are beginning to emerge. Try to buy third or second cutting hay for horses.

♦ Avoid new freshly cut hay as this may be indigestible. Newly made hay needs to cure in the barn for at least six weeks before it is suitable for horses.

♦ If you have the storage space buy a large quantity at a time. This will save money and provide a consistent diet for your horse. When buying large quantities it is a good idea to have a chemical analysis run on the hay to obtain an estimate of crude protein, fiber and digestibility. The county extension agent should be able to assist with this.

♦ Buy by weight. Hay bales can vary considerably in weight and the only way to ensure value for money is to buy according to weight not number of bales.

Types of Hay

Grass Hays

May contain one or more of the following: timothy, smooth bromegrass, orchard grass, rye grass, fescue, coxfoot and a variety of other regional grasses. A lot of this hay is of good nutritional value and very palatable.

Legumes

Includes alfalfa and the several varieties of clover, red clover is considered to be most suitable for horses. Legume hays contain a higher percentage of proteins and minerals than grass hays. In the past, large quantities of legumes were thought to be too rich for horses however, recent research has found no evidence to support this.

Often the best kind of hay to purchase is a mix of grass and legume. Depending on the type of horse and the work being done, the percentage of grass to legume can be adjusted.

HARD FEED

Hard feed is the grain that is fed to provide energy and maintain condition. Deciding what type of feed to buy is often confusing for the first time horse owner. Basically hard feed comes in five forms: straight grains, textured feeds, pellets, extruded feeds and feed blocks.

STRAIGHT GRAINS

OATS

Oats are often the first feed product that comes to mind when the subject of horse feeding is discussed. Oats are an energy giving food containing protein. They can be purchased crushed, rolled, bruised, steamed and whole. Any form of treatment to oats will increase their digestibility by about four percent. Steaming reduces dust in the oats. Processing will add pennies to the cost of any grain and this should be considered when deciding what to feed.

If your horse does not chew his feed correctly, treated oats will aid digestion but you may consider switching to a different kind of feed that is more easily digested.

Oats can be unsuitable for ponies and excitable horses, however they remain an excellent feed for horses in medium to hard work.

BARLEY

A wonderful product for putting on weight barley is rich in carbohydrates. The grain itself is very hard, and for this reason it is best to buy either crimped or rolled barley. Whole barley can be boiled for three hours and then cooled. This produces a warming stew (and a very nasty saucepan!) which is excellent for putting on weight or making a bran mash (see bran.) Feed boiled barley in small amounts (1-3 lb. per day) as it sits heavily on the stomach.

In areas where barley is produced it may be cheaper than oats. Barley is slightly higher in protein than oats but otherwise has a similar feeding value.

CORN

Corn is popular in the western states as a horse feed. It has a higher protein content and a lower fiber content than oats and barley. Corn is considered a good energy producing feed and is useful for putting on weight. Feed with caution as some horses become excitable on straight corn.

BRAN

Before refining processes became so efficient, bran - the by-product of the wheat milling process - was a source or protein and salts. The bran that is available today as a horse feed has had most of the nutritious flour removed from it and is of a lesser quality than before mechanization. Bran still has a place in many horse's diets as a bulk fibrous feed. When fed dry it will have a binding effect, when fed as a bran mash it has a mildly laxative effect. Many people feed a bran mash on the night before a day off or on a weekly or twice weekly basis. The reason for this is as a preventative measure against colic.

MAKING A BRAN MASH

In my opinion the art of making a good bran mash is rapidly dying. For a mash to be appetizing it should be the consistency of bread crumbs and served warm. Boiled barley or boiled linseed may be added although this is optional. Here's how to make a good bran mash:

◆ Put two or three quarts of bran in a bucket.

◆ Add a handful of salt.

◆ To increase the laxative effect and add a shine to your horse's coat add a cup of corn oil or boiled linseed or barley.

◆ Mix in sufficient boiling water until the consistency is that of fine bread crumbs.

♦   Important: Wrap the bucket in heavy sacking or bury it in a pile of hay and cover with several layers. This will allow the bran to cool slowly and as it does it will cook. Allow to cook for at least thirty minutes before serving. Serve with a little sweet feed, molasses or carrots for a tasty meal on a day off or for a sick horse.

All straight grains should have a label on the sack detailing the percentages of minimum protein, maximum fiber and minimum fat. Read the labels because these percentages vary from brand to brand. If you wish to feed a supplement straight grains do not provide the best medium with which to do so. Often the supplement will be left at the bottom of the bucket after the horse is finished. Adding water or molasses may solve the problem.

Straight grains keep better than mixed feed because they lack molasses and added fat which attract flies and go bad during hot weather. Quality is fairly easy to judge by examining a handful of grains for dust and size.

TEXTURED FEEDS

Often called sweet feed, textured feeds have become increasingly popular with horse owners. Textured feed is a pre-mixed horse feed containing a variety of ingredients. Oats are often the main ingredient. The rest of the mix is comprised of corn, barley, bran, soybean meal, molasses and vitamins and minerals. Often the vitamins and minerals are formed into a small pellet which a finicky eater may leave at the bottom of his bucket.

Read the label attached to the bottom of the bag to find out the protein, fat and fiber levels. There are many brands on the market, which offer a wide range of feeding options, including feed formulated specifically for brood mares, young stock, performance horses and breeding stock.

Textured feeds do not keep as well as straight grains. Plan to use them up in two or three weeks, but if an antioxidant has been added they can be stored for as long as five weeks. In hot weather they tend to attract flies and turn moldy. In cold weather they clump together and are difficult to feed.

The price of a textured feed is determined by its major ingredient, often oats. When selecting a textured feed look at feeds that are not oat based. These are sometimes cheaper and provide all the same elements as the oat based feed.

PELLETS

Pellets are another pre-mixed horse feed with the ingredients being ground before being combined into a pellet. This makes pellets more easily digestible and therefore suitable for a horse that does not chew his food well or an older horse with teeth problems. The product is easy to feed and most horses like it. As with textured feed, pellets are available with 10%, 12% and 14% protein. Usually the 10% protein is suitable for a horse in moderate or slow work. The higher protein feed stuffs are designed for competition horses, race horses and breeding stock.

Complete pellets combine fiber with the ground grains, the idea being that the pellet will provide all the horse's nutritional needs and eliminate the need for hay. In theory this is true, however, the horse's digestive system needs fiber in large quantities to maintain correct digestion and hay is always needed.

EXTRUDED FEEDS

These are made from a mash of grains, vitamins and minerals which are heated and mixed together. This mash is forced through a small hole at high pressure to form a nugget. Because of their size these nuggets require more chewing than pellets and may provide better nutrition to a horse that bolts his food (eats without chewing correctly.) They are more easily digested than straight grains because of the cooking and heating of the grains. Extruded feeds are becoming more popular and are often available in specific packages, for example senior and junior varieties. The cost of making extruded feeds adds to their price but it may be worth the extra money to provide a well balanced diet to an older horse or one with special needs. Because of the increased digestibility of extruded feeds, smaller amounts will be needed and this may be more economical than feeding larger quantities of other feed stuffs.

FEED BLOCKS

Similar to mineral blocks in size, these contain a mix of molasses, vitamins and minerals and a high percentage of salt. Most of the nutritional value comes from the molasses. These are not a substitute for a well planned feeding program and at best provide a way to pass the time for the horse. His intake cannot be monitored and these blocks are not to be relied on to provide a well balanced diet. Good hay and access to a mineral block is a much more affordable way to provide a well balanced diet for a horse at rest.

Decide what your horse's nutritional needs are and how many of these needs are being met by pasture and hay. The grain you feed should fill any gaps that are left by hay and pasture. A mature horse doing light work will require very little in the way of grain to provide him with the energy he needs. A horse in training will require more protein in his diet to give him the energy needed to do his job.

The key to good feeding is knowing what the horse is getting and being able to provide what is required based on the horse's age, size, work level and condition. Old time horsemen use their eyes as a guide. When the horse looks underweight increase the feed; when over weight reduce the feed.

SUPPLEMENTS

Supplements are any additives to the horse's diet. Generally horses being fed a complete ration do not need supplements. Supplements can be useful to put weight on a thin horse or to maintain condition an older horse. Be conservative with the use of supplements, in many cases they are unnecessary. This section covers the basic supplements. Always follow feeding directions with supplements.

LINSEED

This is rich in protein and oils. Feed in small amounts as the horse's digestive system can only handle a small amount of oil and the rest will pass straight through. Linseed can be bought as linseed meal, which is ground linseed. Feed only an ounce a day to give the coat a great shine. Alternatively, buy whole linseed and boil it to add to a bran mash. Put a quarter of a cup of linseed in a large saucepan add two cups of water and cover. Bring to the boil and then simmer for five or six hours. This is another saucepan destroyer. If you feed a linseed on a regular basis it is worth investing in a crock pot just for this purpose.

BEET-PULP

Another by-product, beet-pulp comes from the refining of the sugar beet root to make sugar products. Beet pulp comes in two forms - pulp and pellets. It is useful to keep weight on and as a bulk feed. It is very important to soak both kinds of beet pulp for at least two hours. If this is not done the beet pulp will swell up in the horse's stomach. The pellets are mixed with molasses and will require more water than the pulp. Soak a double handful per horse with at least four times as much water. It is better to have too much water than not enough.

VITAMINS

There are many vitamin supplements on the market. If you feel that your horse requires a vitamin supplement try to find an all round one which also contains minerals and electrolytes. Consult your Veterinarian for advice. If you are feeding a balanced diet you may not need any vitamin supplement.

SALT AND MINERALS

These are vital substances for any horse. To ensure that the horse receives as much of these as he needs it is a good idea to provide a mineral block in his stall or pasture. The large ones will last a long time and are worth the money.

ELECTROLYTES

These are needed to regulate sweating and cooling but probably only for horses in hard work in hot weather. Many vitamin supplements contain them so check the labels. Think of them as the horse's equivalent to the popular sports drinks!

During a hot summer day a horse can release up to three gallons of sweat an hour. This sweat not only contains water it but also contains electrolytes essential for bodily functions. The most effective way to replace these is to feed electrolytes with the morning feed on hot days. It is not necessary to feed electrolytes on a daily basis if the horse is not going to be stressed or the weather is not hot. Alternatively, put the electrolytes in the water bucket. This method has the advantage of flavoring the water which will encourage the horse to drink where ever you are.

OTHER SUPPLEMENTS

Go to any tack store and you will find a large section containing additives to improve the coat, increase performance and enhance the feet. Many of these supplements contain vitamins and minerals that you may already be feeding in a basic vitamin supplement. Read the labels. For a horse with special needs consult your Vet, or for feet, your Farrier for their recommendations.

STORAGE

Grain and supplements need to be stored in dry well ventilated areas. They should be kept in horse proof containers to prevent a loose horse from gorging himself. There are great plastic feed bins available or you can settle for a garbage can. Make sure the lid is secured so that a horse cannot remove it. One day there will be a loose horse no matter how careful you are.

Naturally, grain should be guarded against rodents and other pests. If you suspect your grain has been contaminated by insects, rodents, or other pests, do not feed it. It is not worth the risk of colic. A good barn cat is a great asset!

Hay needs to be stored in a dry well ventilated area. If you have a storage area make sure the hay is not sitting on a cement floor which will sweat. Lay down boards so the hay is off the ground and the air can circulate. Lay new hay on edge with a space between bales to allow any heat to dissipate. Keep a large storage area swept and tidy to avoid waste. Have a system for the strings or wires to prevent them accidentally ending up in the stalls. An empty feed bag works well. If you have to buy your hay from the local merchant in small quantities, make sure that it has been well stored and is not damp or moldy. After a couple of loads, a good merchant will know what you like and have it in stock when you need it.

SAMPLE FEEDING PROGRAMS

TYPE OF HORSE				
Fourteen hand pony who is ridden on the weekends by a child. The pony lives out all year round.				
FOOD PER DAY IN POUNDS	**GOOD KEEPER**	**POOR KEEPER**	**EXCITABLE**	**QUIET**
GRAIN	2-4 lbs. pellets	2-6 lbs. pellets or extruded feed beet pulp to maintain weight	2 lbs. pellets or extruded	2-4 lbs. textured
HAY	10-12 lbs.	12-14 lbs.	14-16 lbs.	10-12 lbs.
TOTAL	12-14 lbs.	14-16 lbs.	14-16 lbs.	12-16 lbs.

TYPE OF HORSE

Fifteen hand quarter horse, used for trail riding and local horse shows. In at night and out for 5-6 hours. Ridden five times a week

FOOD PER DAY IN POUNDS	GOOD KEEPER	POOR KEEPER	EXCITABLE	QUIET
GRAIN	4 lb.oats, 2-4lbs. pellets	4-6 lbs. barley, 4-6lbs. pellets, beet pulp	4-6 lbs. extruded, 4-6 lbs. pellets, beet pulp to maintain weight	6-8 lbs. oats, 2-4 lbs. pellets or textured
HAY	14-16 lbs.	16-18 lbs.	14-18 lbs.	14-16 lbs.
TOTAL	20-24 lbs.	26-28 lbs.	24-26 lbs.	24-26 lbs.

TYPE OF HORSE

Sixteen hand thoroughbred used for low level eventing or hunting. Lives in, out for one hour a day. Ridden six days a week.

FOOD PER DAY IN POUNDS	GOOD KEEPER	POOR KEEPER	EXCITABLE	QUIET
GRAIN	4-6lbs. oats, 4-6 lbs. pellets or textured feed	6-8 lbs. barley or oats, 6-8 lbs. pellets or extruded, beet pulp if needed	4-8 lbs. barley, 4-8 lbs. pellets, beet pulp to maintain weight	6-8 lbs. oats, 6-8 lbs. textured or extruded feed
HAY	12-14 lbs.	14-16 lbs.	14-16 lbs.	12-14 lbs.
TOTAL	24-26 lbs.	28-30 lbs.	24-28 lbs.	28-30 lbs.

Chapter Four

GROOMING

WHY DO WE NEED TO GROOM?

As well as to improve the appearance of the horse, grooming is important for a number of other reasons. Grooming is beneficial to both the horse and the horse owner because it allows a bond to be formed between them. To really know a horse's character, it is necessary to spend some time, every day, grooming and interacting with him. Young horses benefit greatly from a daily grooming, because this teaches them to stand patiently, it is also an opportunity for the handler to teach good barn manners and practice leading.

Be in the habit of grooming your horse at least once a day. A little time every day is better than a marathon weekly session. If time is short, go over the whole horse with a brush and clean out the feet. As you do this look out for any signs of injury including new lumps and bumps, cuts, scrapes and skin irritation. When you clean out the feet check the shoes and nails. Check the hoof walls for cracks and anything else unusual. When you take care of your own horse, familiarize your self with his little imperfections (old scars, lumps and bumps) so that you will know what is normal.

Grooming is also important to keep the horse clean and prevent disease. A thorough grooming will remove dirt and scurf from the coat and bring out the natural oils to give his coat a beautiful shine. A dirty coat attracts bacteria and will leave the horse susceptible to skin diseases. Grooming helps to stimulate the muscles and the circulation, which in turn helps to maintain condition.

TOOLS

To groom effectively it is important to have the correct tools. These can be bought at any tack store and most feed stores. Whilst prices and quality vary, a lower priced brush will do just as good a job as a more expensive model. Its not the tools, but how much elbow grease you use that brings up the shine! Brushes come in different sizes, so make sure that you buy brushes that fit your hand and are comfortable to use. Here are the essentials of a grooming kit.

- A rubber curry comb.
- A stiff brush, called a dandy brush.
- A soft brush, often referred to as a body brush.
- Hoof pick.
- Mane and tail comb.
- Sponges for bathing.
- Towels and rub rags.
- Sweat Scraper.

HOW TO GROOM
CROSS - TIES

To effectively groom, the horse must be restrained in some way. Many horses are perfectly happy to stand 'cross-tied' in the aisle of the barn. To make your own cross ties you will need two screw eyes, two lengths of light chain (enough to reach from the wall to the center of the aisle), two light weight 'S' hooks and two single ended snaps. Screw the screw eyes into the wall about 5-6 feet from the ground.

Attach the chain to each and then using the 'S' hooks attach the snaps. Do this on each side of the aisle. The 'S' hooks will either break or open if the horse pulls back suddenly.

Be very wary of cross-ties that have no "weak point," as a horse's natural tendency is to pull against anything that pulls on him. If he pulls back on the cross-ties, he will be fighting the pressure on the top of his head and will not stop until something gives. If the cross-ties are made to secure a charging bull, it may be the horse's neck that gives!

If your horse is worried about being cross-tied you may be able to secure him to a ring on the wall either in the stall or outside. Before tying the horse up, attach a loop of string to the ring (hay string is good for this) and tie the lead rope to the string using a quick release knot. This is again for safety.

A concept that people who are new to horses have a difficult time understanding, is the horse's instinct to run away from anything that scares him. This is derived from the natural "fight or flight" instinct. In their wild state horses were hunted animals, their only defense was to run rarely did they stay to fight. If a horse pulls against a restraint he will continue to pull until something gives. If nothing breaks he will probably panic and injure himself. He is following his natural instinct which is to run. Although you do not wish to encourage your horse to break the cross-ties on a regular basis you do not wish to injure him either. By standing slightly behind (and to one side) of the horse, you can encourage him to step forward should he make a move backwards.

GROOMING

The most important step in grooming is the first step. Picking out the feet. Start by standing on the horse's left side at his shoulder facing the tail. With the hoof pick in your right hand, gently run your hands down the back of the horse's left foreleg and pinch the back of the leg lightly, at the same time asking him to pick it up. Many horses know exactly what you want and will pick up their foot. If yours is a little stubborn squeeze more firmly and lean into his shoulder. With the hoof pick start at the heel of the foot and moving towards the toe dig out all the packed-in dirt. Clean out around the triangular frog, (don't forget the cleft of the frog which runs down the center of the frog) and make a visual inspection of the sole of the foot, the shoe and its nails. Be observant and aware of what the horse's foot normally looks like. Gently place the foot back on the floor. Repeat the process with the other three feet.

With the rubber curry comb, stand at one side of the horse and begin at the top of the neck behind the ears. The rubber curry comb is used in a circular motion on all the large muscles and fleshy areas. Don't be afraid to rub hard, as it is the rubbing action that loosens the dirt and draws the natural oils to the surface. Go over the entire body with the rubber curry comb being careful to avoid the bony areas of the legs and the face. These can be curried with caution! Use a light touch here. For really muddy horses or ponies with a thick coat use the dandy brush to remove the mud and loosen the dirt.

If you are lucky enough to have access to a horse vacuum, now is the time to use it. Make sure your horse is accustomed to the noise of the machine and to the feel of the vacuum. Vacuum all the fleshy areas moving the head of the vacuum over the coat in the a smooth motion. The vacuum sucks up dirt and sand and loosens any deeply seated dirt. If a vacuum is not available, don't worry, you can still get your horse clean with a little elbow grease!

After loosening all the dirt with the curry comb go over the entire horse with a damp rag. This picks up loose hair and dirt and can be used to remove any stains from the coat. You can use plain warm water, or to really bring out the shine try this mixture. In the bottom of a small bucket put a little fabric softener and pine cleaner, fill the bucket to the top with hot water. Take the rub rag and wring it out so that it is damp. Go over the horse from head to toe with the damp rag. Make sure to clean around the eyes and nose. This mixture works great in areas where horses can roll in sand and fine dirt. The fabric softener picks up sand and dust and the pine cleaner kills bacteria and helps to bring up a nice shine. Some grooms like to add a little rubbing alcohol to their grooming water. This lifts out the dirt and cleans the hair. Another mixture to try is a squirt of baby oil to the water, which leaves a trace of oil on the coat and helps to enhance the shine. Try any or all of these and judge the results for yourself.

Take the body brush and starting behind the ears use long sweeping strokes in the direction of the hair to remove fine dirt and stimulate the skin. This will bring the natural oils to the surface which give you that great shine. Brush the entire horse, and don't forget under the mane, the legs and the stomach!

The mane and tail should be handled with care so as not to pull out or break any hairs. There are several products available which can be sprayed on the hair to make combing out easier. Traditionally the mane should lie on the right side of the neck. If you have a mane which naturally lays to the left it will be more manageable to keep it on that side. Treat the tail with the utmost care to avoid breaking the hairs. Take the tail in one hand and start at the bottom with a couple of inches of hair. Comb this out and then move up a little higher. Progress up the tail this way until the whole tail is combed out. Some grooms will pick through a tail with their fingers to remove bits of bedding and never comb out the tail. The tail will grow thick this way however, it will also be in ringlets which are very hard to get rid of!

To finish the horse off, wet the dandy brush and dampen down the mane. Doing this every day will encourage the mane to lay flat. Take a dry towel and run it over the horse to remove any fine dust and promote the shine.

To do a really good job you will need to spend at least thirty minutes working on your horse. A daily grooming will produce a cleaner horse than a weekly bath. A well groomed horse is something to be proud of, especially if he is the result of your hard work!

TAKING CARE OF YOUR GROOMING KIT

To keep your horse really clean it helps to use clean brushes. As you work on your horse you can clean your body brush on the rubber curry comb and then tap the resulting grease out on the floor. There are also metal curry combs available designed specifically for this job. They are not to be used on the horse! Once in a while wash your brushes in warm soapy water and dry them on a towel or in the sun. They will do a much better job if you take care of them!

BATHING

In his natural state the horse did not have to rely on man to keep him clean and disease free. To remove unwanted hair and scurf he would rub on trees and roll in the dirt. Grooming was a natural process. Bathing never occurred. In modern times we expect our horses to work hard for our pleasure. Especially in summer time a horse will return from work and be wet from sweat. Do not bath the horse in cold weather, because he will take a long time to dry and may catch a chill.

SHOWERING

Make sure that the horse has stopped blowing hard before attempting to wash him (see The Stabled Horse for cooling out.) Many horses enjoy a shower with the hose. Use warm water if possible for his comfort. (Recent research has shown that washing with cold water will not cause health problems, which for many years was believed by horsemen.) Start by hosing the forelegs and working up to the shoulder. If you have a hose attachment set the spray on a shower type setting. Hose the neck as far up as he will let you. Be very careful not to get water in the ears as this is very upsetting to horses. If the horse is very fussy try stuffing the ears with absorbent cotton during the bath.

Shower the whole horse except for the head and tail. To clean the head use a sponge to wipe off the sweat. Use plenty of water and then wipe off the excess drips. Some horses will tolerate the hose on their faces, but watch out for water going in their ears, eyes or nose.

If a hose is not available a bucket and sponge will do just as well. On a sunny day set a bucket of cold water in the sun before you ride. The sun will take the chill off the water and be more pleasant for the horse. Some grooms like to add liniment or Vetrolin (a product designed specifically to be used as a brace) to the water. The liniment may help to relieve any minor muscle soreness, and most have a very refreshing odor!

When the shower is over use the sweat scraper to remove the excess water from the coat. This is used in the direction of the coat to scrape out the water. Towel dry the face, being sure to give the inside of the ears a gentle rub. Dry the elbows and the heels. These are the areas most likely to become chaffed if not properly dried.

The sun is the best way to dry the coat. If there is any kind of chill in the air the horse must be covered with a cooler to prevent him catching a chill. There are many types of coolers available. If you do not have one the horse can be thatched to aid drying. To do this pile hay or straw on to his back, which creates an insulating air layer and absorbs some of the moisture. Cover this with any horse blanket or an old blanket off your bed. This was used a lot when the horse was used as a working animal. If the horse lives out the best thing to do is to turn him out. Yes! He will roll in the mud, however most of it will shake off and he will be no harder to clean tomorrow. Do not turn a sweaty horse out and expect him to be easy to clean! The dirt will stick to the sweat!

FULL BATHS

Full soap baths are rarely needed. Correct grooming will always produce a better coat, however, when time is short a bath will help improve appearance. Some grooms swear by a weekly bath to produce a beautiful horse. Be warned that frequent bathing will strip the natural oils from the coat and cause the coat to become dull and dry. If you happen to be the owner of a gray or palomino, stains will be a part of your life. Usually a damp cloth or a sponge will remove these however, occasionally you will need to give a full bath. Horses of all colors will need their manes and tails washed occasionally to remove scurf and dirt.

To give a full bath, wet the horse all over. In a bucket make up a soap solution. There are numerous special horse shampoos available at various prices. If you are on a budget, Ivory dish liquid will do just as well! Using a large sponge, soap the body being careful to work the soap well into the roots of the mane and tail. Use a lightly soaped sponge to clean the face, and rinse thoroughly with a soap free sponge. After the whole horse is soaped and any white markings scrubbed with a soft brush, rinse thoroughly, using either the hose or a bucket and sponge. Make sure that all the soap is rinsed away, because leaving it on the coat can cause irritation and possibly blistering of sensitive skin. Use the drying procedures detailed above.

SHEATH CLEANING

Periodically male horses will need their sheaths cleaned. Naturally, a substance called smegma is produced in the sheath which if left to accumulate can cause difficulty in urination. The frequency of sheath cleaning depends upon the individual horse and the environment in which he lives. It seems that horses living in sandy areas need to have their sheaths cleaned more frequently. Mares too need to have their teats washed and any build up removed.

There are products available to make cleaning easier. Follow the directions on the package. Alternatively use mineral oil, soap and water to clean the sheath. At best sheath cleaning is not a pleasant job. You can wear latex gloves to protect you hand if you wish. Stand to one side of the horse facing the tail. If you have not done this before have someone hold the horse. Pour a generous amount of mineral oil on you hand and gently enter the sheath opening. Carefully work the mineral oil into the smegma around the entrance to loosen and remove it. When all the smegma is removed from the entrance work your way up into the sheath. Be liberal with the mineral oil as this will soften and loosen the smegma. Clean around the penis and gently loosen and remove any dead skin. Some horses will "drop down" when you do this and make cleaning really easy. The final area to clean is inside the end of the penis. Sometimes smegma can accumulate at the end of the urethra forming a bean. Gently slide a finger inside the flap of skin at the end of the penis to search for and remove the bean if necessary. Once the sheath is cleaned apply a little soap to all areas to remove the mineral oil and then rinse thoroughly. Most horses will not object to a hose being used and this can be carefully pushed into the entrance so as to thoroughly rinse out all the oil and soap. For a really dirty horse apply the mineral oil a day ahead of cleaning in order to soften the smegma. Do not forget to soap and rinse the next day as the oil, over time, will attract more dirt.

CLIPPING

If your horse is stabled and regularly sweats during the winter months, consider clipping as a means of reducing both his and your workload. Once clipped the horse will require blankets to replace his coat. A clipped horse will require less grooming than his shaggy counterpart, simply because he does not have as much hair.

Clipping is usually done as soon as the winter coat has come through. Horses can be clipped until New Years without the risk of damaging their spring coat. When clipping is done after New Years there is a chance of damage to the summer coat, the result being a horse that looks clipped all summer.

Clipping is done with large horse clippers. The secret to a good clip is a clean dry horse. If the weather is mild bathe to remove all dirt and grease from the coat. A thorough grooming will also help. If the horse is dirty the clip will be rough and there will be many "tramlines." A dirty horse will wear the clippers out much faster and dull the blades more quickly. Start with sharp blades and test the temperature of the blades frequently as they can heat up. Push the blades against the hair and maintain a light even pressure with the clipper head. It should not be necessary to push the clippers against the skin, the blades should do the work.

Clip the body first and progress to the legs and head. A small pair of animal clippers are useful to do the head, ears, heels and other hard to reach areas. Small clippers are useful year round for trimming whiskers and fetlocks.

There are many styles of clip. The horse can be clipped all over, the legs can be left on or taken off. The saddle area may be left for protection, it can be saddle shaped or simply a round where the saddle sits. A trace clip removes the hair from the belly and underside of the neck. The legs and most of the head is left. This style is useful for a horse that spends a lot of time outside. Clipping is convenient, but remember to keep a clipped horse warm. A hairless horse can catch a chill very quickly!

Chapter Five

HORSES AT PASTURE

Nature designed the horse to live outside and roam long distances in order to find food and shelter. Today this is no longer practical and the horse has become a domesticated animal. In order to produce a faster or stronger horse, man has bred selectively and created many animals that simply would not survive if turned out on the range.

Horses are still generally happier outside and with a little care will thrive. Horses that spend a lot of time indoors may develop stable vices, for example, weaving, cribbing and stall walking.

FEEDING

During the growing season on a large well maintained piece of land, it is possible for horses to need no supplemental feeding, as long as their work load is light. This is true during the summer months when the weather is good. It is also true for ponies who may have to be restricted in their intake.

Let your eyes be your feeding guide. If your horse looses weight, increase his grain ration. Conversely, if he is becoming too well rounded, cut his ration back. During a moderate winter horses can live outside provided that they are well fed and have water and shelter. As a general rule, a horse will need 25% more grain in the winter to keep warm. Watch the weather forecast and when a cold snap is forecasted, increase the grain ration before the cold hits so that your horse is ready to keep himself warm. Free choice hay is important because the horse creates a lot of his body heat from the microbial fermentation of fiber.

WATER

Clean fresh water must be available at all times. Ideally, a gravel bottomed stream with good access is needed, however, this is not always a reality! Most of the time a separate water supply will be needed. There are many kinds of troughs available, some with their own refilling mechanisms. Choose a trough which will be easy to drain and clean. Many horses like to play in the water so make sure that there are no sharp edges or anything else that could cause injury. In small areas a muck bucket with the handles removed will work, or buckets hung on the fence. Of course, someone will need to be around to refill these during the day. To prevent buckets being tipped up try the milk crate method suggested in the stabled horse chapter.

Winter time presents the challenge of frozen buckets and hoses. If you are planning your own barn, install frost free hydrants to supply the paddocks with water. Buckets are easier to handle if they are only half filled and checked more frequently. It is easier to dump half a bucket of ice than a full one! To make the removal of ice easier, smear the inside of the bucket with a thin layer of Vaseline. The ice will slide right out when the bucket is tipped up! In freezing weather bring hoses inside to prevent them freezing and cracking.

EXERCISE

A horse that is on pasture twenty-four hours a day will get all the exercise that he needs to remain healthy. He will to a certain extent keep himself fit but do not expect him to be ready for long or strenuous activity without a proper fitness program and correct feeding. When working a horse off of pasture, follow correct warming up and cooling out procedures (see page 98.)

GROOMING

Grooming is important for a horse that lives outside. Grooming promotes health and provides an opportunity for any injuries to be found and treated. If grooming is neglected the coat will become dirty and matted, reducing its ability to keep the horse warm and encouraging skin diseases.

SHELTER

Horses that live out year round need shelter in both winter and summer. The greatest threat to a horse's well being during the winter months is a combination of wind, rain and cold. A horse subjected to a cold wind will loose condition very fast. Many horses do just fine in rain and snow provided they are well fed, but when combined with wind, wet weather will wear a horse down.

During the summer months the flies pose the greatest threat, and an escape from the worst of them is needed.

A shelter needs to provide a wind break and a dark dry place to escape from the flies. There are many different ways of meeting these needs. A stand of trees can provide sufficient shelter. Three sided run in sheds are great ways to provide all the necessary shelter as well as a place to feed and groom the horse if no barn is available. When building a run-in shed, construct it so that it is facing away from the prevailing winter winds. A great arrangement to have is access to a stall from the paddock. This way the horse can come and go as he pleases and can be kept in if the owner wishes. When designing a shelter, remember the horse at the bottom of the pecking order will get a raw deal if the shelter is too small to accommodate all of the animals.

FENCING

In addition to keeping horses in one place, fencing also serves as a barrier to people who may wish to go and visit the horse. This is especially true if you live in a well populated area. People who are unfamiliar with horses can easily be hurt, and you, as the horse owner may be liable. A good sturdy fence (especially if it is hot wired) will also discourage strangers from entering the pasture and possibly feeding the horses something poisonous. Fences are also used to define exercise areas, round pens and to keep horses away from areas that contain poisonous plants.

SELECTING A FENCE

The type of fence that is selected depends on a variety of factors:

♦   The type of horse. The bigger the horse, the stronger the fence needs to be! Young horses tend to play harder than older ones and require a sturdier and more visible fence. Consider a double fence between paddocks (with a twelve foot aisle), for stallions (not recommended for the first time horse owner), and valuable show horses. A double fence also stops horses in adjoining paddocks from playing over the fence.

♦   Number of horses in the fenced area. The more horses there are in an enclosed area the stronger the fence needs to be. A large pasture with a few horses will not need as sturdy a fence as a small area will.

♦   Access to shelter and feed. Horses will spend a lot of their time hanging out where they are fed and where shelter from weather and flies is available. The fencing in these areas needs to be stronger than in other parts of the pasture.

- ◆ "The grass is always greener on the other side of the fence." This is always true with horses. Expect them to lean on the fence in order to reach that clump of grass on the other side. If crops are grown in the next field make sure the fence is strong and consider putting in a twelve foot easement. To reduce temptation, trim the grass as short as possible around the perimeter of paddocks.

- ◆ The gate needs to be strong, because this is where the horses will congregate, try to push their way through or even try to jump out.

- ◆ Appearances. Always a consideration. Does the fence need to enhance the property or is it for practical purposes only? Around the barn you may wish to have a good looking fence and on the rest of the property a practical fence will be sufficient.

- ◆ Price. Expect to pay by the linear foot. Building the fence yourself will save money, however, some types of fences, such as high-tensile wire and polyvinyl chloride fences, really need professional installation. Fencing is a major expense so make your purchase decisions based on all considerations, not just the price.

Types of Fence
Post and Board

This is a safe and sturdy type of fence for horses. It is highly visible and enhances most properties. Unfortunately, it requires continual maintenance for broken boards and has a high initial cost. Post and board fencing can have either three or four boards and needs to be treated to preserve the wood.

The boards need to be placed on the inside of the posts so that horses leaning against the fence do not push the boards off the post. This is true for any type of fence. This is also a good idea for riding areas as there will be no projecting boards to catch a rider's knee.

Fence posts can be either round or square. Because of the milling process a round post will be stronger than a square post of the same diameter. Treated softwood posts are more expensive than untreated hardwoods but they will last longer and often come with a guarantee. Any post that is used needs to be treated before it is sunk into the ground.

WOVEN WIRE

Woven wire creates a visible, low maintenance fence. Initial cost is high and the fence may be subject to stretching. Commonly a 1 x 6 inch board is nailed above the wire to define the top of the fence. Alternatively an electric wire can be run across the top of the fence. The gaps between the wire need to be small enough that the horse cannot get a hoof stuck in them. Over time wire will rust and break and will need to be replaced.

DIAMOND WIRE

Set up in the same way as woven wire, diamond wire reduces the risk of horses putting their feet through the fence. A safe, low-maintenance fence with a high initial cost.

PIPE FENCE

When available pipe fence can be affordable, sturdy and low maintenance. For a good fence professional installation is probably required as metal cutting and welding are involved.

HIGH-TENSILE WIRE

A good fence for a large area. High tensile wire requires little maintenance when installed correctly, however, it probably needs to be electrified to be truly effective. Professional installation is required to achieve the correct tension. This is a low visibility fence which is why it is not suitable for small crowded areas.

POLYVINYL CHLORIDE (PVC)

PVC fences come in a variety of styles and colors. All look attractive and require very little maintenance. The disadvantages of this fence are its high installation costs and it is not really suitable for small areas with many horses.

ELECTRIC FENCE

Electric fences can be extremely useful as a stand alone fence or to discourage horses from leaning against other types of fence. Electric fences can be used to divide large pastures for rotational purposes. This is also useful if there is only one source of shelter or water, as this can be included in more than one rotation.

Electric fences come in many different styles ranging from single strands to four strands of electrified wire. Installation of electric fences is fairly easy as long as a few simple guidelines are followed. The most important thing to remember is to avoid shorts. These can be caused by ineffective insulators, tall weeds and broken wire. Regular checks of the fence are vital to ensure that it is functioning correctly. The wire needs to be taut but not as tight as a high tension fence.

Electric fences are relatively cheap and easy to move. They are however low visibility fences and horses will need a training period before they will be respectful of electric fences. To increase the visibility of electric fences, tie small strips of plastic to the fence every few feet.

NYLON AND RUBBER FENCES

These fences are made from byproducts of the tire industry. Strips of nylon or rubber are stretched between fence posts. Tension is important as this type of fence is prone to stretching. These make good durable and safe fences but over time they will stretch and need resetting. In colder climates the rubber and nylon will eventually become brittle and need to be replaced. Avoid any fences with exposed nylon threads which horses may eat causing colic.

BARBED WIRE

Although often used as a fence for horses, barbed wire is not recommended. Tension is hard to achieve. The barbs pose a distinct hazard to horses who are not as smart as cattle with barbed wire. Do not use barbed wire for horses. The resulting injuries are not worth it!

HEDGEROWS

Hedgerows are not often seen in the United States, however, they are very popular in Europe. Hedges not only provide a barrier, they also provide shelter from the wind and to a certain extent rain. Obviously, poisonous plants should not be cultivated as hedges. Suitable hedges include blackthorn and hawthorn. These bushes naturally grow into a hedge and when pruned correctly create a dense solid barrier.

If you are building your own paddocks, don't overlook hedges as an option to enhance your property. They can be planted outside of existing fences or supplemented with electric fence until they are thick enough.

GATES

Buy the best quality that you can afford. Gates receive a lot of abuse and the better built they are the longer they will last. The usual gate is twelve feet wide and hung on a gate post which needs to be set in concrete. The gate post is larger than the standard posts. A gate twelve feet wide will allow an entry for tractors and other equipment. If a small entry is needed for feeding purposes, build a three foot gate into the fence. Discourage climbing over any type of wire fence; it is the quickest way to stretch and damage the fence.

PASTURE MANAGEMENT

Good pasture management requires the removal of all trash and foreign objects from the pasture. A daily inspection of the fence and gate is important to ensure that there are no projecting nails or other hazards. Pull up any suspicious looking weeds before they have a chance to multiply.

If you plan to have the pasture provide some or all of the horse's nutritional needs you will need at least two acres per horse. The land should be fenced so that the horse can be moved from one area to another. Electric fences are excellent for this purpose. Research shows that to obtain maximum grazing potential from the land, horses need to be moved off an area very frequently in order for the grass to recover. Three days to a week is the recommended period for grazing each area. The length of time the horses can remain in one spot will depend on the rate of growth of the grass.

If this rotational system is used, the area the horses vacate needs to be mowed to stimulate new growth. Dragging with a chain link harrow is also needed to break up and spread the manure. Not only will this keep pot holes from developing, it will also help to reduce the parasite population by exposing the larvae to the air and drying them out.

Daily removal of manure will also reduce the parasite population. Manure can be composted in a corner and used as a garden fertilizer. Removing manure daily also helps prevent areas of coarse unpalatable grass and maximizes the grazing available. Manure removal should not be overlooked as an effective means of pasture management.

Some kind of rotational system is needed for all horses, even if the pasture is fully supplemented with hay and grain. Horses are "spot grazers," meaning they will graze certain areas down to the roots while leaving others to become inedible. Even if only two paddocks are available, rotating the horses and mowing and dragging the resting pasture will improve the quality and appearance of the grass.

GRASS

The type of grass selected for a pasture depends heavily on the climatic conditions. It is highly possible that a warm weather variety and a cool weather variety will be needed to provide grazing throughout the year. Types of grass used for grazing are Kentucky bluegrass, orchard grass, bromegrass, ryegrass, clover, bermudagrass, dallisgrass, pearlmillet and tall fescue. A word of warning about tall fescue. Older stands may be infested with an endophyte fungus which produces toxins. These toxins have been associated with prolonged gestation in mares and other reproductive problems. Do not graze pregnant mares on tall fescue. During the winter rye, oat, wheat and barley can be used for grazing.

Grasses to avoid because of their poisonous effect on horses include Sorghum-sudangrass hybrids and sudangrass hybrids and Johnson grass.

Your local agricultural extension service can assist with grass selection and other pasture management concerns.

FERTILIZING

The key to successful fertilizing is knowing what the soil needs. This is done by conducting a soil test. Soil testing kits and information about the grazing in the local area are available from your local extension agricultural agent.

Soil testing needs to be done every two to three years and a fertilizing program designed around the results. Lime will be needed to reduce the acidity of the soil and supply calcium and magnesium. It is also important to ensure the efficient uptake of other fertilizer elements. Fertilizer is available in different combinations of nitrogen (N), phosphoric acid (P_2O_5), and potash (K_2O).

POISONOUS PLANTS

There are literally hundreds of plants that are poisonous to horses. The best way to avoid poisoning is to eliminate all unwanted plants from the horse's environment by pulling them up, applying weed killers, and fencing them off. A horse that is well fed will avoid many poisonous plants. Most cases of poisoning produce violent and unpleasant symptoms and in many cases there is no antidote for the specific poison. A poisoned horse will have dramatic symptoms depending upon the type of poison. Respiratory failure, staggering, depression, convulsions, paralysis are all symptoms associated with poisoning. If poisoning is suspected, call your vet immediatly, this is an emergency.

SOME POISONOUS PLANTS

Azalea	Milkweed
Arrow grass	Nightshade
Black Walnut (shavings)	Rhododendron
Black Locust	Russian Knapweed
Bracken Fern	White Snakeroot
Field horsetail	Wild Cherry Trees
Hounds tongue	Wild Tobacco
Johnson grass	Yellow sweet clover
Laurel	Yellow star thistle(very
Locoweed (very common)	common)
Lupines	Yew

DAILY ROUTINE

Although a horse that lives outside requires less time commitment than a stabled horse, he should not be forgotten. Check outside horses at least twice a day. Once a week inspect the paddock fences, gates and shelter. Be on the look out for any trash or poisonous plants and remove any hazardous objects.

Exposure to the elements can leave a horse susceptible to some skin diseases. Every day check the animal thoroughly for these conditions.

SUNBURN

Chestnuts and grays are particularly prone to sunburn. Watch any areas where pink skin is exposed to sunlight. To prevent sunburn apply sun block. On light colored horses check around the eyes and nose for signs of burning. If the horse does get burned use an aloe based cream or any product designed for human sunburn relief. For horses that are very fair skinned use a fly mask to protect the face.

TICKS

In areas where ticks are prevalent check the horse each day. Remove and kill ticks (crush or drown.) Horses can contract Lyme disease the same as humans so it is important to be vigilant during tick season.

MANE AND TAIL RUBBING

If you find your horse rubbing his mane or tail investigate further. First try washing the mane and tail with an iodine shampoo, it may just be dirty! Check for lice by looking for the eggs (nits) attached to the long hairs. Your vet or the local tack store should have powders or medications to control a lice infestation. If itching persists suspect sweet itch. The exact cause of this disease is not known, but it seems to relate to the insects at dawn and dusk. If possible keep the horse in during these hours and talk to your vet about the possibility of shots to help with the itching.

RAIN ROT OR RAIN SCALD

Horses that are not groomed regularly may develop scaly patches on the top of their backs and lose the hair in that area. This is caused by a fungus that is activated by wet conditions. Some areas have more cases of rain rot than others and owners need to be on the look out for the tell tale scabs. Wash the area with an iodine based shampoo, remove as many scabs as possible and dry in the sun. Treatment may need to be repeated for several days. To prevent rain rot keep your horse clean with regular grooming.

MUD FEVER

Similar to rain rot this condition occurs on the legs and is caused by wet muddy conditions. Move the horse to a dry area and treat the same as rain rot. If left untreated can lead to inflammation and lameness.

Chapter Six

THE STABLED HORSE

The stabled horse requires a lot more time than does his counterpart living exclusively at pasture. The stall must be cleaned at least twice a day and someone must be responsible for bringing all his water, food and clean bedding. Each day he must be out of the stall for a period to exercise. This can be in the form of turn out or riding or preferably both. Horses that spend long hours inside soon become bored and develop stable vices. It is healthier for the horse to be outside but, this is not always possible and we must provide the best possible alternatives that we can.

THE STALL
SIZE

The stall is where the horse will spend the majority of his time. It is important to make the stall as comfortable as possible. First consider size. Twelve feet by twelve feet is the standard size for stalls. This will comfortably accommodate a small horse. A larger animal will need a larger stall in order to be comfortable (fourteen feet by twelve feet or larger.) If you are building a barn at home plan ahead. This may be your first horse, but down the road you may buy something larger or even want to breed your mare. If that is the case, go for the larger stalls. The horses will be more comfortable and be able to move around more easily.

FLOORS

When choosing a floor for a new barn, there are several things that need to be considered. The composition of the floor will dictate how dry and clean the bedding will be. Materials used to build stall floors will have an effect on the time and money spent on stall maintenance. An ideal floor is made of a durable material which will not become slippery when wet. The floor needs to be absorbent and easy to clean. It also needs to be resistant to pawing.

CLAY

Clay is a very popular material for floors unfortunately, it is a high maintenance floor requiring periodic patching. Clay creates a slightly warm floor but as time goes by holes will develop and the wet spot will create a small crater. Clay should be put down over crushed rock or gravel and tamped.

CLAY AND SAND

Usually in the proportions of two thirds clay to one third sand, this mixture allows for good drainage and minimizes the odor problems sometimes associated with clay alone. Patching will be required and the stalls need to be well packed and leveled before the horses use them.

LIMESTONE DUST

Limestone needs to be laid over a six to eight inch base of sand or other well draining material. During the laying of the floor the limestone must be watered and packed. Correctly laid it will be nearly as hard as concrete and will therefore require plenty of bedding. Limestone makes a good low maintenance floor.

WOOD

Once down wooden floors are low maintenance. Railroad ties are great for wood floors. The boards used must be at least two inches thick and treated to reduce rotting. There is a risk of the floor becoming slippery when wet although, this can be reduced by packing the gaps with gravel or clay and using adequate bedding. Wood needs a well draining base such as six to eight inches of sand.

CONCRETE

Concrete is incredibly low maintenance. The drawbacks with concrete are no drainage and cold slippery conditions. Horses can develop leg or feet problems from standing on concrete floors for long periods. These floors are easy to clean and disinfect but will require substantially more bedding than other types of floors.

With all types of floors a concrete or asphalt lip at the front of the stall will help to save the floor from traffic and horses pawing at the door.

ASPHALT

Asphalt is similar to concrete floors in character. An unsealed asphalt floor will provide some drainage and therefore will require a little less bedding. Over time asphalt can peel and separate requiring repair.

RUBBER MATS

Rubber mats are great with any kind of floor. On top of dirt and clay they will reduce the frequency of floor repair. With concrete they create a cushion that is easier on the feet and legs. On all floors less bedding will be needed and stall cleaning is faster. Once cut and fitted to a stall they will last a long time.

Unfortunately, mats are expensive. They are also heavy and tricky to cut and fit. If you decide to buy mats go for at least 5/8" thickness. Rubber mats have been available for many years and recently plastic mats have been developed.

I would recommend mats as a way to save your horse's legs and the floor. They may save enough in bedding costs and time to make their purchase worthwhile.

BEDDING

Bedding provides a cushion for the horse, it encourages him to lie down and prevents jarring on his feet and legs. Bedding reduces drafts and allows urine to drain away from the horse, it also prevents hock or elbow sores caused by laying on a hard floor. There are many types of bedding, but these are the most common.

STRAW

Straw should be bright in color and not dusty. Wheat, rye, oat and barley straw are the most common types. Straw makes a good bed and once laid is fairly low on dust. Some horses have a taste for straw and will eat their bedding. Eating large quantities is not recommended and can lead to colic. Of all the beddings, straw is the bulkiest and this may be a consideration if disposal is a problem.

SAWDUST

One of the most economical forms of bedding. Sawdust should be dry and well seasoned. Watch out for chunks of wood that arrive with the sawdust and discard these. Over time sawdust will breakdown into a dusty powder which is useless as a bedding material. Frequently, you can pick up a truck load at a time from the sawmill and save on delivery costs.

WOOD SHAVINGS

These make an excellent bedding as they are dry and low in dust but are more expensive than sawdust. If you are not near to a sawmill these are available in bales.

PEAT MOSS

Darker than sawdust or shavings this is an expensive form of bedding. Peat moss is very absorbent, but is dirty and has a distinctive boggy odor.

SHREDDED NEWSPAPER

In some areas this is available in bales. It is a dust free bedding although disposal maybe a problem.

MUCKING OUT

The stall needs to be cleaned thoroughly once a day and the droppings removed or picked up as often as possible. By getting into the habit of picking up each time you enter the stall you will save bedding and have a cleaner environment for your horse. Less manure will, during the summer months, mean less flies.

Once a week take a broom and knock down the cobwebs. Cobwebs trap dust and if allowed to accumulate become a fire hazard.

WORKING AROUND THE HORSE

It is easier to remove the horse whilst you muck out his stall. If this is not possible spend a little time training him where to stand so he is not walking around and getting in your way. Most horses are pretty smart about this and soon learn to cooperate. It is an important thing for them to understand so they will move out of your way when you go in to pick up the droppings or refill the water.

Put on a halter and stand the horse up against the wall. It is useful to remove hay and feed so you have his complete attention. With the horse against one wall you should be able to clean one side of the stall. If he tries to move tell him whoa and if necessary put him back where you want him. A tap on the chest with the handle of the pitch fork is good to remind him to stand. Clean one side of the stall then move him over and clean the other. Good stall manners are important for all horses and it is up to you to teach and maintain these.

TOOLS

Stall cleaning will be made easier with the correct tools. The correct kind of pitch fork for the type of bedding used, not only makes cleaning more efficient, it is also easier on your back. For straw a five pronged fork is best. The piles can be picked up and tipped into the muck basket without wasting much of the straw. Sawdust, shavings, peat moss and shredded newspaper need a fork with many tines close together. The metal forks are very heavy but the newer plastic forks such as "The Future Fork" are easy to handle.

Wheel barrows are the easiest way to transport soiled bedding. Light weight fiberglass models work well. Muck buckets are good for picking up during the day and a handy three wheeled cart is available to make their movement easier. Manure sacks or sheets can be used. These are spread in front of the stall and the manure piled on. They are closed and dragged or carried away by two people. This can be hard work!

A shovel is always useful for picking up piles in the aisle, and of course a broom or two (these wear out.) For a dirt floored barn a rake is needed and is sometimes useful in the stalls to loosen packed down bedding. Individual circumstances will dictate what other tools will be needed.

HOW TO CLEAN A STALL

The first step is to remove the visible piles. With all kinds of bedding some of the manure will be hidden or mixed in with the bedding. Start in one corner and throw the bedding up against the wall. The manure will fall out and can be removed. Straw needs to be shaken a little to release the manure. Any soiled bedding should be removed as it is found. Work all the way around the stall until all the clean bedding is up against the wall. The wet bedding needs to be removed from the wet spot. If the horse is not in the stall, the floor can be left to dry for a while. Use the broom or rake to remove all the bedding from the wet spot and sprinkle lime on the area. This aids the drying process and helps to deodorize the stall. Use the bedding against the walls to cover the floor. Sawdust and shavings can be dragged down from the walls and smoothed out. Straw will need to be shaken to get it to lay flat. The more straw is shaken the easier it will be to work with. If new bedding is needed it should be piled up against the walls to form banks. These help prevent drafts and may prevent the horse from rolling over and getting stuck against the wall (cast.) Once a week throw all the bedding to the center of the stall and clean the floor areas against the walls to prevent the walls rotting.

Stall cleaning needs to be done everyday to ensure a healthy environment for the horse. With practice you should be able to do a good job in about fifteen minutes or less if the horse is a clean one!

A Cast Horse

A horse is said to be cast when he is unable to get up. This usually happens in the stall when he rolls over and his legs come up against the wall. Unable to get his legs under him or roll back to the other side, he is stuck. Young horses may do this when they are first brought into the barn, but an experienced older horse has usually learned his lesson!

Building large banks of bedding will give the horse a little more room to maneuver and may protect him from injury. To help the horse it is necessary to either slide him back so he can get up or roll him back over. Either way this is dangerous as his legs are waving around in the air and he is probably scared. Several strong hands are often needed. Have someone sit on his neck or head to restrain him and reassure him. You will need a couple of lengths of soft rope. Lead ropes hooked together will do. Carefully pass one rope around his foreleg at the elbow and one around his hind leg. Coordinate pulling efforts and attempt to roll the horse back over. Sometimes he may just be moved enough to be able to get his legs underneath him. As soon as he is able to get his legs in a better position, drop the ropes and get out of the way as he gets up.

For a horse who persistently gets cast there is the anticast roller. This is a roller with a large metal loop at the withers which makes it impossible for the horse to roll over and become cast.

STALL FITTINGS
WATERING

All buckets and mangers should be securely attached to the wall. They can be bolted to the wall or hung by double ended snaps to screw eyes on the wall. When setting up a stall consider where to place buckets to make the work as easy as possible. Water buckets usually work well near the door so they can be easily observed and refilled.

Some stables are equipped with automatic waters. There are several different styles available, which cut down on the tedious chore of hauling water. The best type of automatic water is made by Nelson. It consists of a stainless steel bowl which refills on a tilting system. This kind is preferable because the water can be turned off and the bowl removed for cleaning. Other types of automatic waters rely on the horse to press a lever to refill the bowl. Most horses learn this very quickly however, some will flood their stall playing with the lever. This type can be hard to clean. The disadvantage of automatic waters is not knowing how much water the horse is drinking. This is important to monitor when a horse is sick or stressed, in order to avoid more serious problems such as impactions and colic.

If buckets are used they should be scrubbed out once a day and kept topped up throughout the day. Some horses take great pleasure in dumping their buckets and flooding their stall. To prevent this try using a bucket insulator. This is a plastic holder which is bolted to the stall wall and holds the bucket. These are designed to keep water from freezing in the winter but they work very well to prevent buckets being tipped over. If an insulator is not available, a plastic milk crate will do the same job!

The days are gone when horses were taken to the water trough twice a day in military style. A stabled horse will need clean fresh water at all times. Horses are picky about their water and all watering containers need to be kept clean.

FEEDING

The horse can be fed from a bucket hung on the wall, a plastic feed tub or a rubber tub on the ground. Use whichever you prefer but remember to scrub out the container regularly.

Ideally, feed hay on the ground. This is a natural position for the horse to eat and avoids the risk of dust or seeds getting into the eyes and nostrils. There may be more waste this way, but if you know the horse, you will not feed more hay than he needs.

Hay racks prevent the hay from being trodden on and wasted, however the horse will be forced to eat with his head up in the air and risk dust etc. falling into his eyes and nose.

Haynets are great for weighing hay and soaking if this is needed. They must be hung high so that the horse will not get his foot caught as he empties the net and it begins to sag.

A stable kept horse will need to be fed at least twice a day, early in the morning and late in the afternoon. Scrub and disinfect feed tubs once a week using a mild pine cleaner and remember to remove any uneaten food before the next meal.

For most horses hay should be available at all times. Once you get to know your horse, you will learn how much to feed avoiding waste but keeping the horse happy.

VENTILATION

Proper ventilation is essential for a healthy horse. The air in a barn needs to be constantly changed to remove odors and to prevent respiratory ailments. This can be achieved by windows, fans and roof ventilation.

Stable windows should be designed to open at an upward slant to direct air over the horse. Windows must always be protected with iron bars. If the stall has a half or Dutch door, the top half should only be closed in extreme cold.

During the hot summer months many owners put fans up to help keep their horses cool. Hang the fan where the horse cannot play with it and be extremely careful with the placement of electrical cords.

To draw air up into the roof, creating air flow, the barn should be equipped with some kind of roof ventilation. If hay is to be stored in the loft space make sure there is ventilation to prevent the hay from overheating. Louver boards need to be slanted so that rain cannot enter and always be open. Fans and other devices installed in the roof will create circulation of the air below.

Do not under estimate the importance of good ventilation. A badly ventilated barn will have a damp odor to it and is unhealthy for horses. Horses are not as sensitive to temperature changes as we are. Closing the doors on the side of the prevailing wind and leaving the other doors open often provides ventilation without drafts.

LIGHTING

Stall lights need to be protected with covers or wire frames. The best kind of lighting is florescent tubes. Lights make all stable chores easier. They should be well wired and switches kept out of the way of horses who love to play with them. Avoid the use of extension cords as these are hazardous to have laying around. Lights are needed both in the stalls and the aisle.

CARING FOR THE STABLE KEPT HORSE

Stable kept horses require a fairly large daily time commitment just to care for their needs. This is seven days a week three hundred and sixty-five days a year. Whether you do most or all of the work yourself is a decision that you must make. The point is that you are responsible for arranging someone to do all the necessary chores.

By confining a horse to a stall we take away his ability to provide certain things for himself. These need to be replaced by the next closest thing.

CLOTHING

Stabled horses often require blankets to provide protection from the weather and insects. During the summer months fly sheets will protect a thin skinned horse from insects and help to keep the coat clean. In winter time many owners choose to clip the winter coat in order for the horse to perform without the burden of a fur coat. This will make the work easier for the horse and will make cooling out quicker. The removed hair must be replaced with blankets when the horse is resting and turned out.

There are many different styles of blanket available today. The basic wardrobe consists of a cotton sheet, a heavy blanket for use in the stall, a turn-out blanket, an anti-sweat sheet or scrim and a wool cooler. Depending upon the weather these can be combined to provide the correct temperature for the horse.

If a horse is warm after exercise the anti-sweat sheet will help to cool him without creating a chill. On a cold day, a wool cooler over the sheet will help to wick away moisture from the skin and prevent chills. Always be sure that the horse is completely cool and dry before putting on his heavy blankets. Test how cooled out he is by sliding your hand under the anti-sweat sheet and feeling for moisture. If he is dry between his hind legs and around his stifle he is ready for his blankets. Any tackiness to the coat is an indication that he is not totally dry.

At the end of the winter all blankets need to be washed and stored in garbage bags with moth balls. Many tack stores provide a laundry and repair service. If one is not available in your area, blankets can be washed in garbage cans with a hose and scrubbing brush. This is hard work but it is worth it to extend the life of the blankets. Dry blankets on a line or fence. It is important to have blankets completely dry or they will mildew and rot during storage.

BUYING BLANKETS

Purchasing clothes for your horse is a fairly simple procedure. Decide what types of blanket your horse will need. Most probably you will be shopping for a sheet, heavy blanket, turn-out blanket, scrims and coolers. Most blankets can be bought "off the peg" at tack stores and in catalogs. If you prefer, blankets can be made in your colors for a coordinated wardrobe.

Know what size your horse wears. Measure from the center of the chest, along the body, around the buttock to the center of the tail. This measurement in inches is the size of the blanket. Blankets are made in different styles with different ways of securing them. Avoid any blanket that places pressure on the withers and the spine. Blankets come in different cuts around the neck and different depth in the body. You may have to try several different styles to find the one that fits your horse comfortably. Don't buy blankets that are tight in the shoulders as they will rub off the hair at the point of the shoulder. Leg straps are extremely useful for keeping blankets in place, especially turn out blankets.

BANDAGES

Bandages are used to provide protection, support and warmth. They can be used during shipping to protect the legs from knocks and bangs. Bandages are handy to have available to apply dressings to cuts and wounds or to hold an ice pack in place.

There are many different varieties of bandage available. Decide why you need bandages and then look for bandages that will suit your needs. If bandages are only needed to apply ice packs, old ace bandages will do just fine.

Bandages used as standing or shipping wraps should be used over a bandage pad. These too come in several different styles and densities. Their function is to disperse the pressure of the wrap evenly over the leg. They are applied in the same way as the bandage, wrapping from front to back. Roll the pad up before applying, to ensure an even pressure.

When applying bandages follow these guidelines:

♦ Wrap the leg from the front to the back. Keep the roll of the bandage nearest to you and unroll as you go. Maintain an even pressure all the way around the leg, not so tight that it will reduce circulation but not so loose that the bandage will slip down.

♦ Use pads under bandages. These help to disperse pressure and reduce the risk of a bandage bow.

♦ Practice bandaging; the more you do it the better you will be. If you have never bandaged before, find someone who knows how to bandage properly show you the correct pressure and techniques.

♦ When removing bandages do not roll them up as you go. Pass the bandage from hand to hand, working as quickly as possible. Removing bandages this way is quick and reduces the chance of the horse moving around with a bandage hanging off his leg. The bandage may be rolled up after it is removed from the leg. To remove a tail bandage grasp the top of the bandage and pull down, sliding the bandage off the tail.

♦   Do not leave a bandage on for more than twelve hours. Remove the bandage and rub the leg to restore circulation. If necessary the bandage can be reapplied.

♦   If you doubt your ability to apply a bandage correctly, do not bandage until you have sought help. More damage can be done by a badly applied bandage than by leaving a leg open.

EXERCISE

Due to his confinement the stable kept horse is unable to exercise himself. To avoid boredom and the possibility of stable vices, he needs plenty of exercise. Turn out can often be the answer. The longer the better. Even in a small space the horse will be happier than in his stall. Hay can be fed outside if there is no grass to nibble on and during the winter months this will probably be needed.

If turn out is limited or not available the horse must be ridden, lunged or exercised in some way. It is important to his health to get out of his stall every day. If for some reason the horse must be confined, due to bad weather or injury, cut back or eliminate his grain ration. Feed bran mashes and be watchful for any signs of colic or other illness. When work is resumed, gradually increase the feed and start out with slow work building back up to galloping and jumping, etc.

During bad weather evaluate the footing. Be especially cautious if the ground is icy, slippery or very muddy. A long walk is more beneficial than short trots or canters when the footing is questionable.

WARMING UP AND COOLING OUT

When the horse is first brought out, his muscles will not be warmed up and in a state ready for fast hard work. Many people like to turn the horse out before riding in order to loosen him up and allow him to let off steam if he wishes. This is a great idea and will cut down your warm up time. Before asking for any kind of strenuous work such as galloping, jumping or barrel racing spend at least twenty minutes hacking around quietly. Slow long trotting and large circles are good for warming up. Build up to your chosen activity. This not only prepares the horse for his work but also reduces the risk of strains and sprains on muscles, tendons or ligaments.

When you are finished with the hard fast work, allow the horse to cool down slowly. Watch horses playing in the field. After the hard playing, they spend a while cantering slowly around then trotting and finally walking. They are cooling themselves out. When your horse has done his work for you it is your job to cool him out. Allow him to stretch his neck and walk on a loose rein. This should be done until he has stopped puffing and if the weather is cool until any sweat has dried. Take him back to the barn the way he left. Cool, quiet and relaxed. In hot weather it is not always possible for the sweat to dry and a cool shower and walking in hand will make this stage of cooling out a lot quicker.

During hot summers be very aware of over exerting your horse. Look for signs of exhaustion which include excessive sweating, an increased respiratory rate and a long recovery time. The heart rate will also be increased. If your horse does not recover within thirty minutes and appears depressed, he may be severely exhausted and will require veterinary attention.

Before riding on a hot day take a minute to calculate the relative danger. The formula is:

RELATIVE DANGER EQUALS

Temperature (ºF) + relative humidity - wind speed (mph)
For Example:

$$80 + 70 - 10 \text{ mph} = 140 \text{ (safe)}$$

Under 150 and it is safe to work the horse.
Between 150 and 170 proceed with caution.
Over 180 it is best not to ride or stress the horse.

GROOMING

The stable kept horse needs to be groomed daily. When out in the field horses will scratch on fence posts and trees removing dead hair and loosening dirt. Nature will give them sufficient coats to protect them from the weather. When we bring them indoors they loose this natural grooming system and need to be taken care of.

After feeding conduct a quick groom sometimes called quartering in order to remove the worst stains and check the horse all over for injuries. Many grooms will run their hand down each leg first thing in the morning to inspect for heat and swelling which may indicate the beginning of a lameness problem. Pick out the feet and inspect the shoes.

Before riding, thoroughly groom the horse again being alert for any new injuries. Upon returning from exercise remove sweat and saddle marks. If the horse is sweating a shower is needed. Remember, to scrape off the excess water and dry his head and legs with a towel. If his back is just wet, sponge it off to remove the sweat, and rub vigorously with a towel.

When feeding at night, check the horse over one more time. Remove any "watermarks" with a brush and make sure the horse is comfortable.

LATE NIGHT CHECK

Most well-run boarding stables arrange for someone to check the horses before going to bed. This may be as simple as a quick walk around the barn to make sure that all is well or it may involve feeding hay, picking up the droppings and filling the water buckets. If your horse is at home this is a rather pleasant nightly ritual. A cast horse will sometimes be found at this check and the situation righted. For the horse owner it provides the peace of mind that his horse is comfortable and safe for the night.

Stable Vices

As convenient as it is having a horse readily available in a stall, it is not always a healthy environment for the horse. Long hours in a stall can lead to a number of habits, ranging from the annoying to the down right dangerous. It would be fair to say that most vices and habits a horse has developed are due to mismanagement and unfortunately neglect or even cruelty. If there is no apparent reason for a new habit look for physical causes, pain can cause unexplained behavior and when the pain is relieved the habit ceases. Ignorance is as common an occurrence as abuse. There is no reason for a horse to develop bad habits if all his needs are provided for. When buying a horse be on the look out for stable vices; know what you can live with and what is unacceptable.

Kicking

Horses kick because they are bored, irritable, bad tempered or bothered by insects and other pests. Some horses kick at feeding time in anticipation, and some to keep others away from their food. The walls of the stall can be padded with mats or stall cushions to reduce the noise. For a habitual kicker consider using hobbles or kicking chains. Kicking chains are leather straps which attach around the pastern and have a short chain, which swings back and hits the legs when the horse kicks. These may work for some horses.

Turning the horse out and increasing exercise may help to reduce boredom. If the horse is merely bad tempered, consider if you have the skill and patience to break the habit or at least live with it without getting hurt. Also, consider the damage the horse may do to himself, especially to his hocks.

Stamping and Pawing

Caused by the same things as kicking and also impatience and colic. A horse that is frequently fed by hand will paw to demand his treat. These habits can usually be remedied when the cause is removed or the routine changed. For a hard core offender consider hobbles or kicking chains. Unless a horse is persistent about stamping these vices are not usually a serious problem.

BITING AND SNAPPING

A horse that nips in play and is not disciplined may learn to bite to get attention. In some horses hand feeding can lead to biting and snapping. Irritants like insects and hard grooming can cause a horse to snap.

Young horses often nip and this needs to be dealt with on a daily basis. If this segment of the horse's education is neglected he will see nothing wrong with biting when he is older, in order to assert his authority and get attention. A confirmed biter needs to be handled with extreme caution. Always leave a leather halter on the horse and make sure he is restrained when being groomed and handled. I do not recommend a first time horse owner buying a horse that is known to bite. These horses need to be carefully re-educated and this is a job for someone with a lot of experience.

An occasional nip is to be expected, however, the horse should receive a sharp slap on the side of the muzzle or, if he tends to be head shy, on his chest. Do not hand feed a nipper as it will only make him worse. Avoid hand feeding any horse, it is easy to create a habit , not so easy to break one. Treats can be placed in feed buckets.

CRIB BITING AND WIND SUCKING

These vices are basically the same thing. A cribber will grasp a solid object between his teeth, arch his neck and suck in wind. A wind sucker has perfected his technique and does not need the support of a solid object. As the air is sucked in the horse makes a distinctive burping sound. By swallowing a lot of air the horse will upset his digestion and suffer from colic and excessive gas. A cribber will often be a hard horse to keep weight on because of his continual impaired digestion. Cribbers will eventually wear their front teeth down making grazing difficult. When buying a horse take a look at his front teeth for signs of wear.

Cribbing is usually caused by boredom or by copying another horse. It is a good idea to isolate a cribber so that the other horses do not learn the habit. Once established cribbing is virtually impossible to prevent. The horse must have his fix. A cribbing strap fastened around the thinnest part of the neck will prevent him from arching his neck and swallowing air. This is the only satisfactory method to control a cribber. Cribbing may be reduced by plenty of turn out and exercise however, cribbers will always find something to crib on. Painting the surfaces of the stall with a foul tasting substance may help. There are products at the feed store which may work or you can try hot sauce. Some horses actually like these noxious substances so some experimentation may be necessary. Avoid poisoning the horse!

A horse that cribs or wind sucks is considered unsound. With careful management a cribber can provide many years of usefulness however, buyer beware. Some cribbers carry more weight and condition than others.

WEAVING

A weaver shifts his weight from one foreleg to the other and back again. As he gets into it, he will swing his head left and right and appear unable to stop. Again boredom is the primary cause although some highly strung horses will only weave when someone is in the barn. In this case nervousness is the primary cause.

Plenty of turn out and exercise may reduce weaving. Bed the stall deeply where the horse stands to weave. Eventually the habit will become a nervous disorder and the continual stress on the forelegs probably will cause lameness. A weaver cannot be sold as sound.

If the horse has to be in, provide free choice hay. Weavers get little rest and maintaining condition is often a problem. The hay may also alleviate boredom. Try hanging tires or plastic bottles filled with water over a half door to discourage weaving, these make good toys and by hanging them over the door they may be in the way of the weaver. A confirmed weaver will weave behind a closed door and even weave when turned out. Weaving is another habit which horses can learn by copying, so isolating a weaver is a good idea.

WHERE TO KEEP YOUR HORSE

There are many different situations in which to keep a horse. Boarding stables, shed rows, pastures, small family run stables, and home, are just some of the alternatives to consider when deciding where to keep your horse.

Your other personal responsibilities must be considered when looking for a place to keep your horse. Plan ahead. Do you take regular lessons at a stable? Can you keep your horse there? If not, can they recommend somewhere? Are you planning to do all the work yourself? If so, you must consider how easy is it to get to the barn or pasture. Remember the horse will need to be fed and checked at least twice a day. If you plan to board and pay someone else to do the work, what hours are you allowed to ride? Many boarding stables are closed on Mondays and have limited hours when you can ride. Look at your own situation and decide how much you wish to participate in the day-to-day care of your horse. Bear in mind that the less you do, the more you will pay someone else!

Be sure to ask a lot of questions about boarding agreements. Sometimes lessons are included as part of the boarding agreement. If you choose not to use these will you still be paying for them? Find out if routine vaccinations, shoeing and worming are included. Sometimes these are offered and the cost added to your bill. You may be able to save money by buying your dewormer from a discount catalog and selecting your own Farrier.

Many boarding stables establish their own de-worming and vaccination programs and have all the boarders adjust to their schedule. This is not a bad idea. Not only do you know that your horse is kept up to date on his vaccinations and de-worming you also know that all the horses at the stable are regularly de-wormed and vaccinated, ensuring a healthy environment.

Inquire about other extras. Some stables will charge for turning your horse out and bringing him in. Wrapping, unwrapping, clipping and trimming may all be extra. Make sure you know exactly what the additional charges are before deciding on a stable.

CHECK IT OUT

Whether you decide to board your horse at a local barn, or rent stalls and/or a paddock there are some basic things to look out for.

At first glance what is your impression of the facility? Look out for peeling paint and algae stains on the outside of buildings. Check to see what kind of shape the paddock fences and the pastures are in. Your first impression should be one of order and organization. It does not matter if the buildings are old as long as they have been well maintained.

Have the owner or manager show you around. Ask to see the stalls and look to see if the bedding is clean and the stalls have been recently picked up. One little secret I learned from one of our boarders is to check the state of the water buckets. If these look like they are regularly cleaned and refilled there is a good chance that the horses are well cared for.

Check the quality of the hay, and try to find out how much is regularly fed. Look at the feed room for cleanliness, organization, and the absence of rodents. Inspect the tack room. Is the tack clean and put away, or is it hanging on the cleaning hooks covered in dirt and grease? How does the tack room smell? A well kept barn will have a tack room that smells of leather and saddle soap, not mold or sweat.

Look out for signs of old or dangerous electrical wiring. The excessive use of extension cables will contribute to the fire risk. There should be fire extinguishers in visible, easily accessible places. All light fixtures should be covered. Notice how much light there is. If your horse is to spend most of his hours inside it is important for his health for the stall to be well lit.

Ventilation is very important. Drafts should be avoided but plenty of fresh air is required for a healthy horse. For a horse who spends most of his days in a stall it is a good idea to have some view of the outside world. This will help to reduce boredom and thus the chances of stable vices developing.

Ask to see the paddocks and find out exactly how much time your horse will be allowed to be out. If turn out time is limited, you will have to plan to have the horse exercised each day.

Take a look at the current residents as they will tell the story of a well kept operation. The horses should be interested in their surroundings and visitors. Their coats should be shiny and the horses well rounded and contented looking.

BOARDING CONTRACTS

Boarding contracts can vary from an agreement to pay the specified charges to a more elaborate document detailing responsibility. Do not be afraid of a long contract (in fact you might want to insist on one.) It provides protection for the stable, the horse owner and the horse.

Each state has its own laws and it is a good idea to have a lawyer review your boarding contract. Items included in a typical boarding contract are cost of board and exactly what is included with the basic package. Extras that your horse will need such as shoeing, de-worming and vaccinations and who is responsible for providing these services should also be covered.

A very important area to detail in the boarding agreement is how emergencies will be handled. Horses are experts at getting hurt and sooner or later your new horse will require treatment of some kind. Who has authority in the case of an emergency? Do you wish to be notified immediately or do you trust the stable to make the right decision? What happens if you are unreachable and the horse needs emergency surgery? Cover these eventualities before they happen. Agreements should address as many circumstances as possible. Appoint someone to make decisions for you in your absence. Set an upper limit for veterinary expenses.

If your horse is insured, the company, policy number and telephone number should be given to the person in charge of the stable. Insurance companies require prompt notification of injuries and illness in order to process a claim. In cases of fatal injury or illness they need to be informed before the horse is humanely destroyed.

Use the following check list to evaluate the boarding stables and other facilities that you are considering.

BOARDING STABLE CHECK LIST
NAME:
ADDRESS:

PHONE:

CHECK LIST

First impression	☐ Good	☐ OK	☐ Unacceptable
Stalls	☐ Good	☐ OK	☐ Unacceptable
Water buckets	☐ Good	☐ OK	☐ Unacceptable
Feed room	☐ Good	☐ OK	☐ Unacceptable
Tack room	☐ Good	☐ OK	☐ Unacceptable
Quality of feed	☐ Good	☐ OK	☐ Unacceptable
Quality of hay	☐ Good	☐ OK	☐ Unacceptable
Quantity of hay fed	☐ Good	☐ OK	☐ Unacceptable
Electric wiring	☐ Good	☐ OK	☐ Unacceptable
Fire extinguishers	☐ Good	☐ OK	☐ Unacceptable
Ventilation	☐ Good	☐ OK	☐ Unacceptable
Lighting	☐ Good	☐ OK	☐ Unacceptable
Appearance of horses	☐ Good	☐ OK	☐ Unacceptable
Emergency plans	☐ Good	☐ OK	☐ Unacceptable
Riding facilities	☐ Good	☐ OK	☐ Unacceptable
Paddocks	☐ Good	☐ OK	☐ Unacceptable
Fences and shelter	☐ Good	☐ OK	☐ Unacceptable
Turn out time	☐ Good	☐ OK	☐ Unacceptable

COSTS

Weekly/monthly or daily board	_____
Deworming	_____
Vaccinations	_____
Shoeing	_____
Lessons	_____
Extras i.e. clipping trimming and laundry	_____
Additional charges	_____
TOTAL	_____

Chapter Seven

YOUR HORSE'S HEALTH

FINDING A VET

Just as doctors specialize in a specific area of medicine, Veterinarians usually have one field which they specialize in. The American Association of Equine Practitioners (AAEP) can provide you with a list of vets in your area that specialize in horses (see appendix.) It is well worth the time to find a Vet who understands horses, and possibly has his own. He will have a much greater understanding of your problems than a small animal Vet and will know how to handle a horse. Building a good relationship with an experienced equine practitioner will afford you access to their expertise and in the long run will save you money.

Once you have established a good working relationship with a veterinarian treat them as you would any other professional.

RECOGNIZING A HEALTHY HORSE

Maintaining your horse's good health is all part of being a good caretaker. A healthy horse reflects the care bestowed upon him and is a credit to his owner.

How do you know if your horse is in good health? Take a look at him. Look at the overall picture first.

♦ He should be well rounded with a shiny coat that lays flat.

♦ His expression should be one of contentment not a worried or nervous look.

♦ When he walks he should take even steps and not favor one leg.

♦ His manure should be neither too soft or too hard. It should be of a uniform consistency with the color ranging from green to dark brown. There should be the usual quantity although the size of the piles may vary.

♦ He should urinate without straining and the urine should be pale yellow and cloudy, not dark.

♦ He should be eating and drinking well and when at rest you can barely see the rise and fall of his sides as he breathes.

♦ There should be no discharge from his eyes or nose, and he should not be coughing.

♦ He has no unusual lumps, bumps or wounds.

♦ At rest he should not be sweating or agitated.

If all the above are satisfied the horse is probably in perfect health. When one or more of these conditions are not satisfied something is wrong with the horse. In time you will be able to tell immediately if something is not quite right with your horse. Frequently it is something simple that can be quickly remedied before a more serious condition develops. If you observe any abnormal behavior investigate further. A good place to start is with the horse's temperature.

Taking the Temperature

Your first aid kit should include a veterinary thermometer. Attach a length of string through the ring of the thermometer and to the other end of the string attach a clothes pin. Shake the mercury down into the bulb of the thermometer. Apply Vaseline or some kind of lubricant to the stem of the thermometer. With one hand gently pull the horse's tail to one side. Insert the thermometer into the rectum using a gentle twisting motion. Attach the clothes pin to a handful of tail hairs. Wait at least two minutes. Remove the pin and grasp the end of the thermometer, and with a twisting motion gently remove the thermometer. The horse's normal temperature ranges from 99°F - 101°F (38°C). A temperature over 102°F is abnormal. A higher temperature may indicate a serious illness. Note: After exercise and eating the temperature will be naturally higher. Temperatures are usually higher in the evening than in the morning. Always take the temperature when the horse is at rest for an accurate reading. It is a good idea to take the temperature of your horse on a regular basis so that you have a norm to work from.

A temperature higher than 102°F indicates fever and will most likely require veterinary attention. If the temperature is normal observe the horse for other signs of distress, including rapid breathing, patchy sweating and anything out of the ordinary. If you are unable to treat the horse yourself make notes of any symptoms you observe and be ready to describe them to the Vet in detail. Remember you are the one who knows the horse best. Your observations will greatly assist the Vet in his diagnosis.

Fortunately most injuries will not require such drastic action. The diligent horse owner will be able to deal with many minor injuries himself. A basic first-aid kit, stored in a convenient place is a must for all horse owners.

EQUINE FIRST-AID KIT

The kit listed is a starter kit, it is useful to have at the barn to take care of minor injuries. As time goes by you will accumulate other veterinary supplies such as poultices and specific ointments.

Veterinary Thermometer,
Absorbent Cotton,
Gauze pads,
Hydrogen Peroxide,
Rubbing alcohol,
Ice packs,
Epsom salts,
Sharp scissors,

Vaseline,
All-purpose ointment,
Furacin is very popular,
Wound powder,
Bandages and pads for
wrapping the legs,
Adhesive Tape.

WOUNDS

Wounds can range from a minor scrape to deep gashes or puncture wounds. When treating a wound it is important to evaluate the severity of the injury. If upon close examination the wound appears to need stitches call your Vet immediately and then follow the wound treating procedures below. Do not apply any kind of dressing as this will make stitching difficult.

TREATING WOUNDS

If there is profuse bleeding this must be stopped. Cold hosing may reduce the blood flow to the area and aid in clotting. Applying pressure to the area or just above it will also help to stem the blood flow.

The wound must be cleaned, and if much swelling is present cold must be applied to reduce the swelling. Cold hosing works to clean the wound as well as reduce swelling. A simple cleaning can be done using iodine soap and absorbent cotton to clean out the wound. Clipping the hair away around the wound may assist in keeping the wound clean. For small minor wounds use hydrogen peroxide. If a foreign body is suspected in the wound, i.e. a piece of wood from the fence, avoid rubbing the wound as this could push the object in deeper. The Veterinarian should remove the object, the wound may be cleaned by cold hosing until he arrives.

Depending on the type of wound select either wound powder (to dry up the wound) or ointment (to protect and moisten the wound.) For a swollen area it will be necessary to apply cold to the area two or three times a day until the swelling subsides.

Follow up includes keeping the wound clean and applying the dressing of your choice.

HOT AND COLD THERAPIES

Hot and cold therapies have been used for many years by horsemen to treat wounds. Cold is used to decrease circulation and therefore swelling. Heat will increase circulation and blood flow supplying the area with natural healing substances. Alternating the two extremes will often help to accelerate the healing process. Usually cold is used until the initial swelling has been reduced. Heat is used to promote circulation or draw out pain and infection.

COLD THERAPY

Legs are the most susceptible area and are the easiest to treat. Cold hosing is very effective, though if a hose is not available an ice pack can be applied and secured with a bandage. Select a thin bandage and bandage over the affected area. Place the ice pack on the bandage and bandage over the pack. You can save your ice packs and reuse them. A bag of crushed ice will work as will a bag of frozen peas or corn, as long as you have practiced your bandaging. There are also special boots available for applying cold to the legs. These are expensive and the same result can be achieved with a freezer pack and bandages. Apply cold therapy for twenty minutes at a time and repeat until the swelling is reduced. This may take two or three days. Three times a day is probably enough for most wounds. With most kinds of swelling the horse is better off moving round. Turn him out if possible to help reduce the swelling and prevent stiffness.

HEAT THERAPY

Heat is needed to draw pain and infection out of wounds. Abscesses and some kinds of lumps can benefit from heat treatment. Vaccinations sometimes cause a reaction resulting in a hard bump. Heat can reduce the pain and break up the lump before it becomes permanent. Applying heat can be as simple as soaking the foot in a tub of water to draw out a foot abscess. For lumps and other injuries requiring heat there are several options.

Hot fomentations can be applied. With a bucket of hot water mixed with Epsom salts apply a wet towel to the area. Wring out the towel and hold it against the wound. When it begins to cool, dunk it in the bucket again.

Another option is to use a hot pack that can be heated in the microwave. Be careful not to over heat this. A hot pack can be bandaged onto a leg and left for twenty minutes. It is a good idea to apply a thin sheet of cotton over an open wound to prevent irritation.

If a microwave is not available make your own hot pack using bran, hot water and a zip-lock bag. Mix up the bran and hot water and seal it in the bag. This can be held to the area or bandaged on. Bran holds the heat very well and will last for twenty minutes if it is covered.

POULTICING

This may be necessary to reduce heat and bruising. In the case of swelling in the lower leg, poulticing will help to relieve the swelling and pin point the exact site of injury.

There are many different types of poultices available all of which do a reasonable job of drawing heat out of a wounded leg. Poulticing is a messy job and it is a good idea to have all the equipment assembled before you start.

You will need a tub of poultice, a bucket of water, a towel, bandages and pads and either brown paper (cut out of a feed sack) or saran wrap. If using paper cut it so that it will wrap around the leg easily and then put it in the water.

In order to avoid blistering the area be sure to wash any medications off of the leg prior to poulticing or sweating. Wet your hands and apply the poultice liberally to the leg. Be generous with the poultice because it works by absorbing the heat from the leg and thus relieving the swelling. A thin film will not absorb much heat. Rinse any excess off your hands and wrap the paper or saran wrap over the poultice. Finally apply a bandage pad and bandage. A well done poultice will work for twenty-four hours, although it may be necessary to reset the bandage after twelve hours if it has slipped at all.

Upon removal note how dry the poultice is. If it is caked on it has drawn a lot of heat and a second one is probably needed to continue the job. The easiest way to remove a poultice is to scrap off any excess and return it to the tub for future use. The remainder can be hosed off and the leg dried.

SWEATING

A sweat can be used to break up a long standing lump or one that is not responding to other treatment. Furacin is a common sweat, although there are many different things that can be used to sweat a leg. Talk to the Vet about what he prefers to use.

To apply a sweat smear the ointment all over the area to be sweated. Wrap saran wrap around the leg smoothly and as wrinkle free as possible, and then apply a standing bandage. Leave the sweat for twelve hours or overnight.

TYPES OF WOUND

CLEAN CUT

Clean cut wounds are caused by a sharp edge, this wound has smooth edges. Initially there may be a lot of bleeding, however once this is stopped, they generally heal quickly.

TORN

The edges of a torn wound are rough and jagged, often being caused by a blunt object. Bleeding is usually not a problem though these wounds can be hard to clean and healing may take a while. Hosing may help if there is a lot of dirt and dried blood.

With both clean cut and torn wounds a large gaping wound may need stitching. If this is the case call the Vet immediately as an old wound cannot be stitched. Large wounds will leave a scar and, if looks are important, a few stitches are called for. A deep wound will heal much faster with stitches and be less trouble. Evaluate a wound as if it was on your own arm and take the corresponding action.

BRUISES

Bruises are most often caused by blows, knocks and kicks. These appear as swellings and may be accompanied by heat and pain. Minor bruises usually take care of themselves. A large swelling will require treatment to hasten healing as the swelling must be reduced. This can be done by cold hosing, applying an ice pack and by the use of anti-inflammatory drugs which your Vet can prescribe.

PUNCTURE WOUNDS

Puncture wounds are the most dangerous kind of wound. The wound is deeper than its entrance. Usually caused by long sharp objects entering the flesh. The danger with a puncture is infection, caused by the entrance closing and trapping dirt and bacteria inside. The key to successfully healing a puncture wound is for healing to occur from the inside out. Keep the wound open by flushing with water and hydrogen peroxide and prevent it from scabbing over. Drainage is essential for the wound to heal completely (if a puncture drains excessively suspect a foreign body.) Consult your Vet for deep puncture wounds. Frequently he will advise an anti-tetanus booster as a precaution.

Be especially careful with puncture wounds near to joints. If the wound has penetrated the joint sac the joint may be affected and this can be very serious. If in doubt consult with your Vet.

SCRATCHES

Sometimes called cracked heels, these lesions occur at the back of the pastern. They are caused by damp conditions including; wet muddy paddocks, heavy dew fall (called dew poisoning) and humid conditions during the summer. Whenever you bathe or shower your horse it is important to towel dry the back of the pasterns. The skin in that area is sensitive to moisture and if not properly dried will develop dry scabby cracks. Chestnuts and horses with white legs are especially susceptible to scratches.

Clean scratches and dry thoroughly. Apply antiseptic ointment to the area, twice a day. Desitin is great for scratches because it seals out moisture. Another good remedy is a mixture of Vaseline and Furacin ointment, mixed half and half. The key to controlling scratches is keeping infected legs clean and dry. Avoid wet muddy paddocks and heavy dew in the mornings. Be sure to always dry the heals after a bath or shower.

INTERFERING

This happens when one leg strikes another causing a wound. Interfering is caused by bad conformation, bad action, a green horse, an overtired horse, a loose clinch and bad shoeing. As with all injuries find and remove the cause. If it is caused by conformation or action, the horse can wear boots to protect his legs.

If recurring marks or wounds appear on the leg, the culprit is interfering. Stand directly in front of the horse and watch how he moves as he walks, then move to the rear and watch him walk away from you. Frequently, it is possible to see the offending foot passing or touching the injured site.

BRUSHING

Brushing occurs when one leg or foot knocks against the other causing injury, usually to the fetlock. The wound can be caused by the shoe striking the opposite leg, in which case the Farrier may be able to shoe the horse to minimize the problem. Brushing boots, which come in many styles, are a good way to protect the legs.

OVER-REACHING

The injury resulting from an over-reach is often called a grab. The toe of the hind shoe strikes the back of the foreleg usually on the heels or at the back of the pastern. Grabs most frequently occur during fast work and in deep going. Bell or over-reach boots will help reduce the number of injuries.

FORGING

The hind shoe strikes the underneath of the front shoe causing a clicking sound, this maybe due to the toes becoming too long. The Farrier can often correct this fault.

UNDERCUTTING

The toe of the front foot scrapes the toe of the hind foot as it lifts off the ground. Associated with compact short backed horses. Corrective shoeing is usually the key to managing this problem.

EYE INJURIES

The location of the horse's eyes make them very prone to injury. Most eye injuries involve bruising around the eye socket. The eye will swell and sometimes close. The danger with eye injuries is damage to the eye itself. The most common kind of eye damage is a scratch or puncture of the cornea.

Take a close look at the eye. For best results try to find a dark place in which to make the examination. If you have a pen light shine it on the surface of the eye. Any clouding of the cornea indicates a wound to the eye and your Vet should be called immediately. Eye infections and ulcers can develop quickly and be extremely painful. The quicker treatment is started the better the prognosis.

If there appears to be no damage to the eye itself gently clean the area with warm salt water. Use absorbent cotton to gently clean and irrigate the area. Swollen eyes should begin to heal in a day or two. If the condition appears to worsen or does not begin to heal within twenty four hours call your Vet. Watch eye injuries closely for signs of deterioration.

All wounds should be evaluated, and if the Vet is needed he should be called as soon as possible. Take care of minor wounds and they will not become a problem. If a cut appears to be infected, contact your Vet who will prescribe antibiotics and advise you on the correct treatment.

HEALTH ROUTINES

Regular vaccinations and deworming are essential for a healthy horse. Keep a notebook to remind yourself when these are due. Also note down any unusual reactions from the horse, such as a sore neck after certain vaccinations.

VACCINATIONS

A good vaccination plan is important to keep you horse healthy. The type and number of vaccines administered will vary from area to area and situation to situation. Horses that travel and are in contact with other horses will require more vaccines than ones that lead more isolated lives. When planning which vaccines to give your horse, take into consideration how much contact your horse will have with other horses and how often he will make a public appearance. Consult with your Vet as he is the person best qualified to advise you, and will administer the vaccines.

Tetanus is always recommended. Horses are very susceptible to this fatal disease, and for this reason a booster shot should be given (in addition to the annual vaccine) following serious injuries.

Encephalomyelitis is also recommended. This occurs in the Eastern, Western and Venezuelan forms and is nearly always fatal.

Influenza vaccine and rhino pneumonitis vaccines are given to most horses. These diseases are not always fatal however, prevention is better than cure!

Strangles, rabies, botulism and Potomac horse fever vaccinations are also available. Your Vet is best qualified to advise you on which vaccinations to give. Frequently, vaccines are available as one mixed vaccination. It is recommended that your Vet be consulted about vaccinations, and administer them in the spring and the fall or the appropriate time for your region.

EQUINE INFECTIOUS ANEMIA

This is a viral disease which has been reported in all parts of the world. The United States Department of Agriculture and all the mainland states have taken steps to prevent the spread of this sometimes fatal disease. Any horse shipping from state to state must have a negative coggins test dated within one year. Many stables require a negative coggins test before a horse is allowed on the premises. The coggins test is named after the Vet who researched equine infectious anemia and developed a blood test to detect it.

The incidence of equine infectious anemia has been greatly reduced by these policies and it is the horse owners responsibility to have his horse tested annually. The Vet will take a tube of blood and send it to the lab for testing. When you ship your horse anywhere it is a good idea to have his coggins test available.

WORMING

All horses carry a number of internal parasites. These are picked up from pasture as eggs or larvae and mature in the horse's intestines. To control this parasitic infestation all horses need to be on a regular deworming program.

The frequency of deworming will depend upon your individual circumstances. Worms thrive in warm, humid areas and do not do so well in arid conditions. The horse population and the methods of pasture management will also have an effect on the number of worms. In areas with many horses and little acreage the horses will need to be dewormed every four to eight weeks. If grazing is plentiful and the paddocks well maintained deworming will be less frequent. The best way to set up a deworming program is to consult your Vet about the conditions in your area and your individual circumstances.

In addition to routine worming there are also products available which can be fed on a daily basis. These have proven to be useful for the control of internal parasites, though, they tend to be more expensive than paste wormers and are not totally effective for young stock.

There are many types of worms that infest horses and they can be controlled by a correct worming schedule. Deworming products are most commonly sold in single dose syringes. There are several brand names available. The important thing to look for is the active ingredient because by rotating the drugs used, the chances of the worms building up a resistance to a single drug is reduced.

If your horse begins to loose condition suspect a large parasite load. Typically a horse with a worm infestation will have a dull coat, his ribs will be showing and he may be pot-bellied. A fecal sample given to your Vet will reveal an egg count indicating the degree of infestation and the types of worms involved. This will aid in the prescribing of anthelmintics (deworming drugs.) For a severe infestation your Vet will recommend an aggressive deworming program. Plan to deworm with a product containing ivermectin in the spring and again in the fall to control bots.

INTERNAL PARASITES

There are many species of internal parasites. These are the most common in the United States.

ASCARIDS

Also known as round worms these are the largest internal parasite affecting horses. Adults can grow to twelve inches in length and be as wide as a pencil. After hatching in the small intestine they do their damage as they burrow through the liver to the lungs. From the lungs they are coughed up and swallowed by the horse to start the life cycle again.

Mature horses develop some immunity to these worms. Foals and young horses are particularly susceptible to Ascarids and may go off their food and develop a cough. A horse with a heavy worm load also develops a pot belly and a rough looking coat.

STRONGYLES

Often called blood worms because they suck blood through the walls of the digestive tract. They can grow up to two inches in length and gather in the arteries slowing the blood flow. A heavy infestation can lead to colic. Strongyles can cause damage to the internal organs by blocking the blood vessels and reducing blood flow.

PINWORMS

Pinworms live mostly in the rectum and appear around the anus to lay their eggs. They are two or three inches long as adults and will cause a horse to rub his tail.

BOTS

The bot fly looks like a small bee and can be found buzzing around the legs. Horses are very upset by these flies and stomp or run from this annoying predator. The bot fly

DEWORMING PRODUCTS

BRAND NAME	FORM	ACTIVE INGREDIENT	EFFECTIVE FOR
Strongid Paste	A paste wormer	Pyrantel pamoate	Ascarids, Strongyles, Pinworms
Strongid C	Fed daily with grain ration.	Pyrantel Tartrate	Ascarids, Strongyles, Pinworms
Zimecterin	Paste wormer	Ivermectin	Ascarids, Strongyles, Pinworms, Threadworms, Bots
Eqvalan	Paste and liquid which can be administered by syringe	Ivermectin	Ascarids, Strongyles Pinworms, Threadworms, Bots, Lungworms
Panacur	Paste wormer	Fenbendazole	Ascarids, Strongyles, Pinworms
Safe-Guard	Paste wormer	Fenbendazole	Ascarids, Strongyles, Pinworms

sprays its eggs onto the forelegs where they appear as tiny white specks.

The eggs will hatch producing larvae which the horse licks into his mouth and swallows. The larvae attach themselves to the stomach wall until spring when they let go and are passed out with the manure to hatch into adult flies. Whilst in the stomach they can cause the stomach lining to be inflamed creating digestive problems.

During fly season remove the eggs daily with a knife blade to break the cycle.

TAPEWORMS

Tapeworms live in the intestines and generally do not cause problems for the horse.

WARBLES

Warbles are more common in cattle than horses, but can cause pain and damage to horses. Similar to a bot fly the warble fly lays its eggs on the legs. The larvae burrow through the skin and migrate throughout the body. They eventually arrive at the back, usually under the saddle, and cause a small painful lump. In cattle the larvae complete the life cycle and mature into flies, but in horses they often die producing an abscess. Treatment often requires the removal of the dead larvae, a job for the Vet.

PASTURE MANAGEMENT

Effective pasture management will assist in the control of internal parasites as well as keeping flies to a minimum. If possible, pastures should be rotated to break the life cycle of the worms. By moving horses to a new pasture every two months and dragging or harrowing the old pasture it is possible to greatly reduce the parasite population.

When space is limited, the worm load can be reduced by keeping the pasture free of manure. Though picking up manure everyday is a chore, your grass will be better and your horse healthier. Even a regular harrowing schedule will help to dry out manure and kill the larvae. Do not underestimate the benefit of good pasture management. It makes both economic and horse sense!

Save one or two empty worming syringes. When washed out they are useful for administering other medications.

Teeth

The horse's teeth are designed for grinding. To compensate for the wear to the chewing surfaces the teeth grow throughout the horse's life. As a result of this growth and the continual grinding, sharp edges develop that can cause discomfort when eating. This in turn can lead to poor condition.

In addition, wolf teeth often develop just in front of the premolars. Wolf teeth have small roots and will often interfere with the action of the bit causing pain whilst being ridden.

Dentistry

All horses should have their teeth checked at least once a year. A knowledgeable dentist can feel if the molars need floating (rasping down the sharp edges) and should be able to do this quietly and efficiently without scaring the horse.

Wolf teeth are most commonly found in young horses simply because theses animals have not yet had any dental work done. Any horse that is expected to wear a bit will need his wolf teeth removed. Again a knowledgeable dentist should be able to do this.

Dentists

Your Vet is qualified to work on your horse's mouth and may be your only option. There are horse dentists who may be able to offer a better service than your Vet because their specialty is teeth. There is no formal training required to become an equine dentist and most have learned their trade by apprenticing. Ask other horse owners if there is a dentist in your area. The local tack store may be able to advise you as may your Vet. Dentists travel a lot and you may be able to fit into a regular schedule if you can wait a few months. Unfortunately, some dentists do a better job than others and are better with the horses than others. Recommendation is the only way to find a good dentist and if none seem to be available trust in your Vet to do the job.

Chapter Eight

COMMON AILMENTS

COLIC

Colic is any type of abdominal pain.

TYPES OF COLIC

Colic falls into two categories: medical colic and surgical colic. The symptoms are similar for each kind. A Vet needs to determine if the horse is a medical case which will respond to treatment or a surgical case that will require surgery. The quicker this is determined the better the chances of recovery. Surgical colic often mimics medical colic by responding to treatment for a period. With surgical colic the symptoms will reoccur indicating that more aggressive treatment is required.

CAUSES

There are many causes of colic and many are related to bad management.

- Over feeding.
- Unsuitable foods such as moldy hay or poor-quality grains.
- Sudden changes in diet or feeding schedules.

♦ Feeding a hot horse or allowing a hot horse to drink a lot of cold water may cause colic.

♦ Parasites when present in large numbers.

♦ Sand in the stomach.

♦ Abrupt stress and/or trauma

SYMPTOMS

From the observable symptoms it is hard to tell which type of colic is occurring. The horse will be distressed and may look round at his stomach. Kicking at the belly and pawing the ground indicate pain and discomfort. Patchy sweating and increased respiration may be present. Frequently the horse will lay down, roll, and get right back up again.

The pain associated with colic is caused by discomfort in the digestive tract. The problem may be a simple case of gas, or there may be an obstruction somewhere in the intestine. This is called an impaction. In some cases, for reasons that are unclear, a portion of intestine will flip over upon itself causing a complete blockage. This is extremely painful and it is these cases that often require surgery.

Sometimes the symptoms are subtle. In this case take the horse's temperature and observe very closely. In all cases call your Vet. This is an area requiring immediate veterinary attention to relieve the pain and correct the problem.

TREATMENT

Treatment should definitely be left for the Vet. If you suspect colic call the Vet immediately. Remove all hay and grain from the horse. The horse may be permitted to lay down although violent rolling should be discouraged as this may cause injury to other parts of the body. It was once thought that rolling may cause a colicky horse to twist his gut. It is now widely believed that the pain causes the rolling and no further danger of twists exist. Walking may be useful to keep the horse quiet but this is not essential.

The Vet will be able to diagnose the severity of the colic by listening to bowel sounds with the stethoscope and by a rectal examination. Administering a large dose of mineral oil via a stomach tube is a standard practice along with the administration of pain killers. Follow any instructions carefully to assist in a speedy recovery.

In the case of a severe impaction or a twist the horse may require surgery. This can be performed at your vet clinic, a state veterinary university, or other facility designed for equine surgery. Your Vet will refer you to the appropriate place. More and more the risks associated with surgery are reduced, although the after care is time consuming and the procedure costly. Currently 60% of surgical colics are still alive after one year. Most colics do not require surgery and correct aftercare will ensure that there is not a recurrence. Try to determine the cause so that it can be removed.

If you live in an area with sandy soil your horse may ingest more sand than it can cope with leading to sand colic. To reduce the sand in his intestine, feed one of the psyllium based products designed for this purpose. The gel that is formed on the stomach picks up the sand and carries it out of the digestive system. Follow the directions on the package.

COUGHING

Coughs can be caused by many different things. If your horse starts to cough it is important to find out what may be causing the cough and remove the cause. An occasional cough is probably not a serious problem but if it persists make a note of when it happens and ask your Vet for his advice.

Coughing is an indicator of inflammation in the airways. Inflammation can be caused by irritation or infection.

CAUSES

Coughs can be caused by bad ventilation or dusty conditions. Dusty fine hay can cause coughing as will moldy hay.

Frequently, parasites are to blame for a cough and these should be dealt with promptly.

Diseases such as flu will cause coughing, and are accompanied by a rise in temperature, nasal discharge and general lethargy. Isolation of the horse will help prevent the spread of the disease. Call the Vet right away.

If a horse has suffered a respiratory disease or has broken wind, (this is a condition which causes the lungs to lose some of their capacity) he may cough or have trouble breathing when stressed. Coughing may be accompanied by an elevated respiratory rate. Observe the horse at rest. Eight to twelve breaths a minute is normal. Look at the nostrils, if they are flaring more than normal this is a sign of an increased effort during respiration.

Allergies can cause a cough. Allergy shots can be formulated for an allergic horse. A series of shots followed by lifetime boosters will protect an allergic horse from the discomforts of an allergy attack.

PREVENTION AND TREATMENT

Prevention is often better than cure. Provide adequate ventilation for horses kept inside. Minimize exposure to dust by turning the horse out when bedding the stall and doing other dusting around the barn. For a horse with a persistent cough the best environment is outside - the only exception to this is a cough caused by pollen allergies. This is the natural place for a horse and the fresh air is beneficial to the respiratory system. This is not always possible and the next best thing is to provide a dust free environment. Ensure that the barn has adequate ventilation and is not air tight.

Moisten the grain before feeding and consider soaking the hay. I say consider, because this is a messy and heavy job. Soaking the hay for approximately thirty minutes and then draining before feeding removes most of the spores and dust which cause irritation. The best way to soak hay is outside in a large garbage can. Put the hay in a haynet and cover with water. After thirty minutes you can tip up the can and leave the net to drain. Try it just once to see how much dirt is left in the water. You will be horrified!

If your horse is not prone to playing with things try feeding the hay out of the plastic garbage can water and all. The soaked spores will be too large to cause a problem and this may save some mess and heavy lifting. Omit the haynet and soak the hay directly in the can.

If this seems like a lot of effort to go to you can try dampening the hay with a watering can. Break up and shake out the hay before dampening. This will not remove all the spores but it might be just enough to prevent coughing.

Keep the stall clean and lime the floor regularly. Ammonia from the urine can vaporize and cause irritation. Lime helps to neutralize this and keeps the air fresh.

Coughs can be troublesome and the causes sometimes indistinct. Try to find and remove the cause. For persistent coughs which are not accompanied by infection talk to your Vet. He may know of a cough going around your area or be able to help with finding the cause.

COLDS
SYMPTOMS

The same symptoms that we suffer will be suffered by the horse. The temperature may rise for two or three days. The horse will sneeze and his eyes and nose will run. Sometimes he will cough.

A cold itself is not serious, however, there may be complications if a horse continues to be worked. Keep him quiet and away from other horses.

TREATMENT

As with a human cold the best you can do is relieve the symptoms. Provide plenty of fresh air, and if the weather is reasonable turn the horse out. Vapor rub can be applied to the nostrils to help clear his head. If coughing is severe your Vet can prescribe medicine to ease this. Rest the horse until the symptoms subside and then gradually bring him back to work.

HIVES

Also known as Urticaria or nettle rash, hives can appear anywhere on the body though they are most often seen around the head and neck, and under the belly. Although alarming, hives are usually not serious.

CAUSES

A sudden change in diet can cause the horse to break out in hives, especially if the change is an increase in protein. Some plants and insects can cause an allergic reaction resulting in hives.

The lumps that appear generally do not cause any irritation and often disappear as quickly as they appeared. The temperature remains normal.

TREATMENT

If the cause is identified and removed the welts will disappear on their own. Sometimes it is hard to remove the cause, as in the case of insects. If these cases do not improve, your Vet can prescribe antihistamines or similar medications to treat the condition.

DIARRHEA

Although not a disease in itself, diarrhea is a symptom which should not be ignored. It may indicate too much rich pasture or a more serious condition. The danger with prolonged diarrhea is dehydration. If the cause is not simple, for example, rich grass or new hay, call the Vet immediately.

CAUSES

Diarrhea can be a sign of enteritis or inflammation of the bowel. In this case the diarrhea will be accompanied by spasmodic pain. Enteritis may be caused by a number of things including: bacteria, unsuitable diet, moldy hay or grain, chemical poisoning, and poisonous plants.

Diarrhea can occur in older horses as their teeth and digestive systems become less efficient. In these cases it is advisable to feed a more palatable diet. Specially formulated feed for seniors is easily digestible and can be moistened to make chewing easier. The addition of electrolytes and vitamins to the feed will aid in the control of diarrhea.

Foals are also susceptible to diarrhea, especially when their mother is in heat. Ask your Vet for the correct treatment for foals.

TREATMENT

Try to find and remove the cause. Your Vet will prescribe the correct medications based on the probable cause. Electrolytes may be added to the feed to replace those lost. It is important to monitor how much water the horse consumes to ensure that he does not become further dehydrated.

BROKEN WIND

Scientifically known as chronic obstructive pulmonary disease (COPD), emphysema or heaves. This is a breakdown of the air sacs within the lungs resulting in a loss of elasticity and reduced lung capacity.

CAUSES

Often the result of an allergic reaction to dust, pollen and fungal spores. Recent research suggests that dust and spores in hay could be the primary cause of COPD. Any kind of strain on the lungs may result in broken wind including: feeding before work, chronic coughing, diseases affecting the respiratory tract, galloping of an unfit horse and dusty conditions.

SYMPTOMS

The first noticeable symptom is a harsh deep cough which gets worse with exercise. Breathing will become more difficult and if work is continued will become labored. The classic symptom of heaves is the double effort required to exhale. This can be observed by watching the flanks. A broken winded horse will appear to exhale twice before each breath.

TREATMENT

Once the lungs are damaged the best treatment is control of the environment. Keep dust to a minimum and if at all possible have the horse live out. Dampen all feeds. The condition can be controlled if it is not too severe, however, there is no real cure and good management is essential.

If the disease progresses it will turn into emphysema and the horse will be severely distressed.

Chapter Nine

LAMENESS

Lameness in the horse is always something to be concerned about. Some lameness' are easily diagnosed as their symptoms are clearly visible, whilst others are subtle and even finding the afflicted limb can be a problem. Stress and strain on the legs caused by bad conformation or excessive work can leave tell tale signs on the legs which will indicate possible weakness. By being familiar with the lumps and bumps that accompany many horses it is possible to make an educated guess at the horse's possible future soundness.

PIN POINTING LAMENESS

Some sites of lameness are obvious, for example, a bad cut and a grabbed shoe are two causes of lameness that are easy to find. Other lameness may not be as easy to detect and a system is needed to narrow down the possible sites of lameness. When searching for the cause of lameness remember that 90% of lameness occurs in the foot.

With a lameness that is hard to pin point start by thinking back. What work did the horse do in the last few days? Has the Farrier been within the last week? Is there any history of lameness which may be recurring? Try to think of anything that may have happened, which may be related to the current problem.

Observe the horse's stance in the stall. Is he resting one leg? If a foreleg is hurt the horse may point that toe (standing with one leg in front of the other.) If both forelegs are sore he may rest one and then the other.

Make a thorough examination of the suspected legs. Feel for heat and swelling and test for pain by gently squeezing any suspicious areas. Lift the leg and move it back and forth looking for signs of resistance. Compare the legs. This is the only way that you can tell if something is amiss. Remember that you are the person most familiar with the legs of this horse. Anything that appears even slightly different deserves further investigation.

Often times the first few steps will be the most telling. A condition which causes stiffness will be most apparent after the horse has been standing for a period. If the horse is in a stall, watch as he makes the step out of the stall and makes the turn. A subtle lameness will often show up at this time.

Jogging or trotting the horse on a hard level surface is the most widely accepted test for lameness. At the trot the lameness will be most apparent. When watching a horse trot, look at his head and the way it moves. With lameness in a foreleg the head will be raised as the injured limb hits the ground. This relieves the weight on that leg and thus reduces the pain. With hind leg lameness, the head will lower as the affected leg touches the ground again to reduce the pain.

Have the horse led away from you and then trotted back, so you are observing the movement head on. If nothing is obvious watch the horse both coming towards you and going away. Move round to the side and watch from the side. Notice the lengths of the steps. They should be equal and free. If the movement is restricted in any way, hone in on this and evaluate this area further.

When trotting a horse for a lameness evaluation, be sure to run to the side of the horse and leave as much room as possible between you and the horse so that the person watching will have an unrestricted view. Avoid pulling on the head. Allow the horse to trot forward and freely with out any interference which may give a false result.

At this point if nothing is found the Vet will be called in to conduct his own investigation. Be ready to give a complete history of the problem and anything related to the horse which may contribute to the lameness. The Vet will perform the tests described above and, if he finds nothing, will also ask to see the horse turned in small circles and possibly lunged.

Turning in a small circle places more stress on the inside legs and may help to exaggerate the problem. Lunging demonstrates the lameness on a larger circle and may make it easier to observe the problem. The Vet can also perform flexion tests on the hind legs and sometimes the forelegs. The principal behind flexion tests is to stress the joints for two minutes by holding the leg in an elevated and cramped position. When the leg is released the horse is immediately trotted forward. Any problem in the joints of the leg will be exaggerated for the first few steps and lameness is amplified.

Do not forget lameness caused by back pain or teeth problems. Sometimes a problem shows up as lameness even though all the legs are fine. The horse cannot talk so he must demonstrate his discomfort in other ways and lameness is a definite sign that something is wrong.

TYPES OF LAMENESS

Leg lameness can be roughly divided into four categories. Foot lameness, diseases of the bone, sprains or strains and bursal enlargements. All of these problems have their own specific symptoms and degrees of seriousness. Foot lameness is dealt with in the chapter "The Foot and Shoeing."

DISEASES OF THE BONE

Bone diseases are usually caused by excessive work, bad conformation and direct blows to the bone. Sometimes they develop over time due to other conditions that the horse may have. There are four conditions from which bones can suffer.

♦   Ostitis. This is a general inflammation of the bone.

♦   Periostitis. An inflammation of the periosteum (the membrane which covers the bone.)

♦   Exostosis. This is the process of laying down new bone tissue on top of old bone. Usually the resulting surface will be rough, often with tiny bone spurs that can cause trouble. It usually occurs with ostitis

♦   Ossification. The transformation of cartilage into bone.

SPLINTS

Splints occur on the cannon or splint bones. Periostitis is caused by concussion or direct blows to the leg. Once they are formed they usually do not cause any trouble unless they are extremely large or are located near a joint. A hard lump forms on the bone and in the beginning, when the splint is active, the area will be warm and often painful to the touch. If the horse is lame the lameness will get worse with work. Cold therapy is needed to reduce the heat and swelling and limit the size of the splint. As the splint is forming, limit the horse's work, to walking and turn out. If the horse is worked during formation of a splint, the splint will be needlessly large.

Splints usually occur in young horses. It is rare to find a new splint forming in a horse over six years old. When buying a horse make a note of any splints. These may have been caused by a blow to the leg or they maybe the result of a conformational defect such as pigeon toes. Always ask the history of any abnormalities. This will enable you to make a better guess at the possible future soundness of the horse.

Old splints can sometimes be reduced by rubbing them with a hard object such as a piece of plastic pipe. Old time horsemen used a chicken bone to do this, it is however the rubbing and the heat created that reduces the splint.

SORE SHINS

Commonly seen in young racehorses, this condition is caused by concussion. First noticed when the horse takes short steps, if forced to continue, lameness will result. Swelling and heat can be observed on the front of the cannon bones and the area is often painful to the touch.

Rest is the best thing for this condition. Initially poulticing will help to reduce the pain and swelling, after a couple of days, cold therapy will be beneficial. When the horse returns to work, hose the legs afterwards to help prevent a recurrence. This is an example of periostitis.

RINGBONE

Ringbone can appear on either of the pastern bones and is commonly caused by excessive stress on the forelegs due to upright pasterns or poor shoeing. If the ringbone occurs near the joint the horse will be lame. Usually heat and pain are minimal and lameness will persist with work. A ringbone away from the joint will not cause lameness. Ringbone involves the process of exostosis - the laying down of new bone.

Treatment consists of cold therapy and possibly corrective shoeing. Veterinary advice is recommended because eventually the bones will fuse causing the horse to be incurably lame.

BONE SPAVIN

Spavins are located towards the bottom of the hock on the inside. They are the result of a bony growth between two of the lower bones in the hock. This fusing of the bones will reduce the flexibility of the joint. A sickle hocked horse or one with very bad cow hocks will be susceptible to spavins.

Excessive stress to the hocks may result in a spavin. Lameness will lessen with work only to return the next day. The affected leg may take shorter strides and the toe may be dragged.

Initially heat therapy will help to relieve inflammation and after a couple of days cold therapy will tighten up the leg. Veterinary advice is needed and possibly corrective shoeing will help.

An occult spavin is a spavin which occurs between the weight bearing surfaces of the joint, i.e. between the bones. This can be a serious problem and often hard to diagnosis.

SIDE BONES

Side bones are the result of injury to the lateral cartilages of the foot. The cartilage ossifies forming bone. Direct injury above the coronet bone can cause ossification of the lateral cartilages. Concussion is another cause of side bones.

Often the only symptom is the bump itself. If no lameness is present no treatment is needed. If the horse is lame, cold therapy is needed until the lameness is gone. Over time side bones can cause the hoof to contract, eventually causing other problems.

SPRAINS AND STRAINS

MUSCULAR STRAINS

Just as a human athlete can pull a muscle so can the equine athlete. Muscular strains can occur if the horse becomes cast, exerts himself too much or makes an unusual movement. Muscular strains can occur anywhere in the body and can be detected by heat, pain and swelling. Unless severe they will heal quickly. Rest will accelerate the healing process as will heat therapy and massage. For a badly pulled muscle, the Vet can help with medication and possible alternative therapies like laser or magnetic therapy.

STRAINED TENDONS AND LIGAMENTS

A strained tendon or ligament is also referred to as a bow. A horse with a bow is said to have "broken down." Tendons and the ligaments that attach them to the bones are fibrous, nonelastic cords. In the event that they suffer more strain than they are capable of bearing, they will stretch and will not return to their original length. Once stretched the tendon will remain stretched and take on a bowed shape. Often some of the fibers will rupture causing a weakness to occur in that area of the tendon. Whichever happens the symptoms and treatment are the same.

Bowed tendons are caused by excessive stress being placed upon the legs. A sudden change of terrain when moving at high speed, too much galloping, pulling up suddenly, and exerting a tired horse can all lead to bowed tendons. Conformation may make a horse more prone to tendon injury. Long sloping pasterns and tied in below the knee are two weaknesses which under the right conditions can lead to bowed tendons. Allowing the toes to become overly long and the heels to drop will add stress to the tendons.

Unless very mild the horse will suddenly become very lame. He will probably want to rest the affected leg and will be unable to continue. Swelling will follow involving the whole of the back of the leg from the knee or hock to the fetlock. Heat and pain will be present. In mild cases the symptoms are limited to heat and swelling in the affected area and a lesser degree of lameness.

Poor bandaging, and wraps that are applied too tightly, can also cause the tendons to bow. It is important to learn how to apply wraps correctly to avoid causing injury to the legs. A bow caused by a wrap is called a bandage bow.

Treatment is prolonged because of the tendons poor blood supply. Initially cold therapy is needed to minimize the swelling from the injury. As soon as the injury is discovered start hosing and call the Vet. The treatment usually involves cold therapy and poulticing until all the traumatic swelling is gone. Rest is important in the early stages to prevent further injury. Once the initial swelling is gone the Vet may advise switching to heat therapy to improve circulation and promote healing. Medications can be used and the Vets advice on correct dosage etc. must be followed. Recent research suggests that a gradual return to exercise aids in the healing process. This will depend upon the severity of the injury and your Vet can help you design a treatment schedule.

A horse that has a bowed tendon will often have thickness in that area of his leg. In bad cases the whole of the back of the leg from the knee or hock to the fetlock will appear to bulge outward. Once set, bows are usually strong. Unless you are shopping for a sport or competition horse do not rule out an animal with an old bow. When buying a horse, or evaluating the severity of a new injury, ultra-sound can be used to view the tendons. This technology is reasonably affordable. Your Vet can perform the procedure or recommend an experienced technician.

CURBS

A curb occurs four to five inches below the point of the hock. A curb is an enlargement of the ligament at the back of the hock joint. Basically curbs are caused by the same things as other strains, however, some horses are predisposed to curbs because of their conformation. When evaluating a horse be especially cautious of sickle hocks.

Treatment is the same as for any other sprain. Corrective shoeing may help.

BURSAL AND SYNOVIAL ENLARGEMENTS

All the joints in the horse's body are enclosed in a protective sac called the synovial membrane. Some tendons and other structures are also enclosed in a bursa which protects them. The synovial membrane secretes synovial fluid some-times called joint oil. When the sac is full the pressure prevents the production of too much fluid. As the pressure drops the cells which produce synovial fluid are stimulated to secrete more. This system can be damaged by injury or excessive strain on the joint. When this happens a swelling will be visible on the outside of the body.

Synovial enlargements often develop as cold painless lumps. If they are caused by a direct injury there maybe heat and pain with the swelling. In this instance veterinary advice should be sought. A swelling which has developed over time is an indication of wear and tear. Most do not cause any trouble and will probably remain with the horse for the rest of his life. When evaluating a horse look for these indicators. They show that a horse has worked but unless accompanied by other problems do not cause a lameness threat.

Treatment will involve the use of cold therapy. An en-largement caused by injury will usually disappear. Long standing enlargements can be temporarily reduced with the use of cold therapy, massage and bandaging. If the enlarge-ment is caused by wear and tear it will generally reappear.

BOG SPAVIN

These appear on the inside of the hock and there may be one or several puffy swellings. Straight hocks are prone to bog spavins. Bog spavins do not usually cause lameness, though the condition may interfere with the action of the joint if the spavin is very large. Corrective shoeing maybe called for.

THOROUGHPIN

Located on either side and just above the point of hock a thoroughpin is a distention of the tendon sheath. A true thoroughpin can be pushed from side to side and is usually caused by stresses on the hock. Although not usually respon-sible for lameness, large thoroughpins are unsightly.

WINDGALLS OR WINDPUFFS

Windpuffs are a very common problem which rarely causes lameness. The swelling occurs above the fetlock on both sides of the leg and may be caused by overly long toes as well as stress from work.

CAPPED ELBOWS OR SHOE BOIL

Capped elbows are caused by insufficient bedding, conformation or the hoof catching the elbow when laying down. The elbow may rest on the ground or may be injured by the hind foot as the horse gets up. Initially the swelling is soft and may be reduced with cold therapy. Once set it becomes hard, and does not usually cause a lameness problem.

CAPPED HOCKS

Similar to capped elbows, capped hocks occur at the point of the hock. Capped hocks can be caused by lack of bedding, kicking the walls or direct injury. Remove the cause, and in the early stages cold therapy will help to reduce the size of the swelling.

CAPPED KNEES

The swelling on the knee is usually caused by a blow which is often self inflicted by banging on the stable door. Remove the cause, and apply cold therapy. Capped knees are not usually a lameness problem.

SITES OF FORELEG LAMENESS

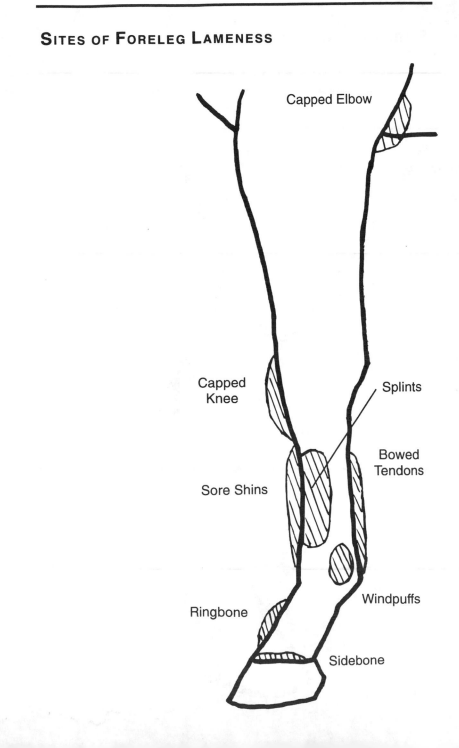

Capped Elbow

Capped Knee

Splints

Sore Shins

Bowed Tendons

Ringbone

Windpuffs

Sidebone

SITES OF HIND LEG LAMENESS

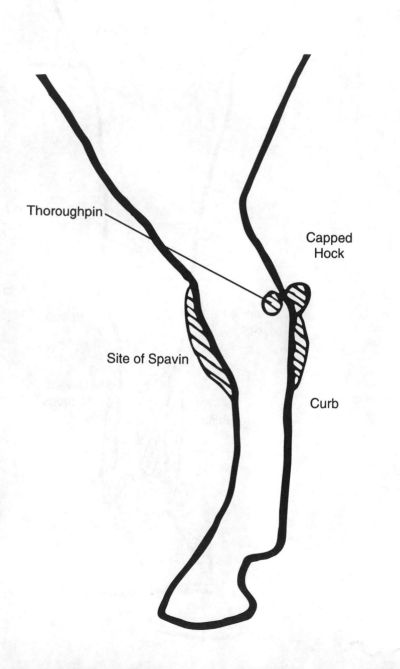

Thoroughpin

Capped
Hock

Site of Spavin

Curb

THE LOWER LEG: INTERNAL STRUCTURE

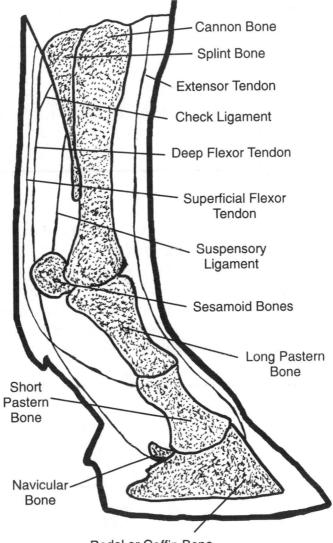

Cannon Bone

Splint Bone

Extensor Tendon

Check Ligament

Deep Flexor Tendon

Superficial Flexor Tendon

Suspensory Ligament

Sesamoid Bones

Long Pastern Bone

Short Pastern Bone

Navicular Bone

Pedal or Coffin Bone

LAMENESS SUMMARY

Lameness is always worrying. Be vigilant and keep a record of your horse's activities. This includes vaccinations, shoeing, visits by the Vet, and schooling sessions. With well kept records it is easy to look back and see what may be causing an unexplained lameness.

FINDING LAMENESS

◆   Check the feet and shoes.

◆   Observe the suspected leg or legs for obvious injury. Feel for heat, pain and swelling.

◆   Watch the horse trot.

◆   Watch the horse being lunged or turning in a small circle.

◆   Consider other causes such as teeth problems, back pain, muscle pulls, badly fitting tack or stiffness after a fall or strenuous workout.

◆   For lameness that has no apparent cause, look at the shoulder or stifle for signs of soreness. This type of lameness is not as common as lower leg lameness, but problems do occur in the shoulder and stifle.

◆   If lameness is intermittent try to find a pattern. This will help the Vet to narrow down the cause.

By continually monitoring the horse's legs for changes it is likely that any lameness or injury will be noticed before it becomes a serious problem. Vigilance is the key to a happy sound horse!

Chapter Ten

THE FOOT AND SHOEING

THE IMPORTANCE OF HOOF CARE

The importance of taking good care of the horse's feet cannot be stressed strongly enough. The old saying, "No foot no horse" still holds true. If your horse is lame, you cannot ride, and he is probably in pain.

Talking to Farriers I have concluded one of the most useful things a horse owner can do is to become familiar with the feet, and be able to tell instantly if something is amiss. In short be observant. Learn as much as you can about the feet and the Farrier's role in maintaining a healthy foot.

Hooves can tell you a lot about a horse. They tend to be a reflection of the horse's environment and can tell you something about the horse's previous care. In humid wet areas the feet will be soft and crumble easily. In dry areas they will become hard and brittle. If stable cleanliness has been neglected the feet may be diseased and in poor condition. Changes in diet, injuries, or systemic diseases will show up in the feet as rings, indentations or flaws in the hoof wall.

Good nutrition is vital for healthy feet. A good diet will provide all the components necessary for the hoof to grow. If your horse has particularly poor feet, there are supplements available which assist in the growth of healthy horn. Your Vet or Farrier can help you determine which product to use.

THE SOLE OF THE HOOF

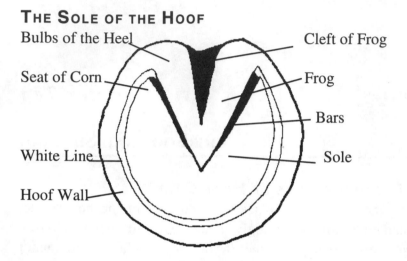

Bulbs of the Heel — Cleft of Frog

Seat of Corn — Frog

Bars

White Line — Sole

Hoof Wall

THE STRUCTURE OF THE HOOF

To appreciate the importance of hoof care it is necessary to understand a little about the structure of the foot. The hoof is a structure made of horn. Horn is hard and does not readily expand. Whenever a hoof is injured the blood supply to the foot is increased. Along with this comes heat and swelling. The increasing pressure and heat cause a lot of pain inside the hoof. To treat many types of foot injuries the pressure must be reduced to relieve the pain. This is why it is vital to take care of the feet and be observant of any changes in the foot or shoes.

CHOOSING A FARRIER

Finding a Farrier who will do a good job for you and your horse is of utmost importance. Farriers are not required by law to be licensed, so in fact anyone could set himself up as a Farrier!

Of course, one of the best ways to find a Farrier is by recommendation. Ask your Vet, riding instructor and other horse owners. Bear in mind that many Farriers specialize in one type of horse, for example, western pleasure horses or dressage horses. It is best to find a Farrier who works on horses similar to yours so that he will understand your shoeing needs.

Be ready to ask a potential Farrier about his work experience and professional qualifications. Many Farriers have attended Farrier schools and apprenticed with an established professional before starting out on their own.

Look for someone who will listen to your shoeing problems and not just stick the shoes on as fast as he can. When you find a Farrier that you can work with - and can work with you - be sure to establish a good working relationship with him. This relationship will be beneficial to you and your horse.

Have your horse ready for the Farrier. This includes not only presenting a horse with clean dry feet but a horse who has good manners. It is not the Farrier's responsibility to train your horse to pick up his feet and stand to be shod. Picking out the horse's feet everyday not only helps to keep the foot healthy it also teaches the horse to pick up his feet and stand whilst they are worked on.

Be available to hold the horse if needed and warn the Farrier of any nasty habits the horse has which may make his job more difficult. Make sure the legs are clean and free of any creams or other medications which the Farrier will get on his clothes. One last thing: don't apply hoof dressing right before he arrives in order to make a good impression!

The largest governing body in the United States is the American Farriers Association (AFA) who strive to certify their members and provide continuing education. Each state or region has a Farriers association to provide an opportunity for Farriers to share their experience and knowledge. The AFA headquarters can provide a listing of all their certified Farriers to assist in your decision (see appendix.) Unfortunately not all Farriers are registered with the AFA and you may well find a good Farrier who has no certification. There are three levels of certification:

INTERN FARRIER

This certificate shows a knowledge of equine anatomy, gaits and shoeing procedures.

CERTIFIED FARRIER

A certified Farrier has been shoeing for at least one year. More knowledge and a deeper understanding of shoeing is required.

CERTIFIED JOURNEYMAN FARRIER

The Farrier has been shoeing for at least two years. An in depth knowledge of anatomy, gaits and shoeing procedures is required, along with the ability to shoe a horse with a set of hand made shoes.

THE FARRIERS TOOLS

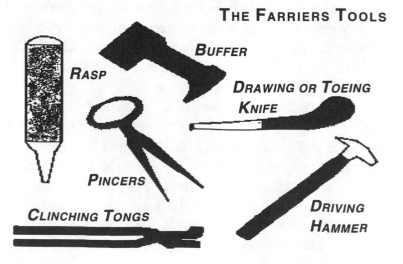

RASP

BUFFER

DRAWING OR TOEING KNIFE

PINCERS

CLINCHING TONGS

DRIVING HAMMER

TRIMMING

Whether you ride your horse or not the hoof will continue to grow down from the coronary band. It takes from nine to twelve months for the hoof to grow from the coronet to the ground. Our domesticated horses will need this growth trimmed periodically. The frequency of trimming depends on many factors including: nutrition, the weather, the horse's work load and health, and the ground that he works on. Your Farrier can advise you as to how often your horse will need to be trimmed, expect somewhere from four to eight weeks between trims.

Trimming removes excess growth from the hoof wall, frog and sole. It is done to prepare the foot for shoes or as a maintenance procedure (similar to us trimming our own nails). If the foot is trimmed correctly the angle of the hoof wall matches the angle of the pastern and the shoulder. If too much foot is removed the horse will be foot sore and tender. Allowing the feet to become too long will cause the foot to become unbalanced resulting in tripping, stumbling and increasing the likelihood of splits and cracks in the hoof. A neglected foot will eventually turn up at the toe, and may break off, causing the horse much discomfort.

SHOEING

REMOVING THE SHOES

It is important for all horse owners to be familiar with the techniques involved in removing shoes. Occasionally a horse will grab a shoe and twist it out of place. If the shoe is not removed immediately, there is a possibility that the horse will further injure himself with the projecting shoe, or even step on an exposed nail. If the Farrier is not close by, the shoe will have to be removed. Many stables have tools specifically for this purpose. It is not necessary to buy a set of tools, however, it is important to know how to remove a shoe. Shoes can be removed using improvised tools such as a screw driver to raise the clinches, a regular hammer and pliers to lever the shoe off. This is not recommended as standard practice, but for emergency use only.

The shoe is removed by holding the foot between the knees and using the sharp side of the buffer to raise the clinches (the turned down nail heads). Slide the edge of the buffer under the clinch and tap it with the hammer to lift the clinch up. If the clinch is very tight use the rasp to create a small groove under it. Work on each clinch until they are all raised.

With all the clinches raised, take the pincers and lever the shoe off starting at the heels and working towards the toe. This is hard work! Watch your Farrier work and ask him to explain what he is doing. This is all you will need to do in an emergency situation. When your Farrier arrives he can fix any rough edges, your job is to avoid further injury. If the shoe is not likely to cause further injury, leave it for the Farrier to remove and keep the horse quiet in the mean time. After removing the shoe the edges of the foot can be wrapped in duct tape to prevent further damage until the Farrier arrives.

PREPARING THE FOOT

After the shoe is removed the Farrier will trim the hoof with the hoof or toeing knife. The excess growth will be trimmed and the ground surface leveled with the rasp. Any ragged pieces on the sole or frog are removed.

FITTING THE SHOES

Most shoes used today are made in a factory. They come in different sizes and your Farrier can adjust them to fit the horse's foot. Hand made shoes are used for therapeutic shoeing and other specialty situations. It is rare to find a Farrier that makes all his own shoes today as this is a time consuming job, and the factory made shoes do an adequate job.

Your Farrier will discuss with you the types of shoes available for your horse and advise you on which are the most suitable. The correct size of shoe is selected and adjusted using the hammer and anvil. Sometimes it will be necessary to heat the shoes in the forge to make a better fit. If this is the case the hot shoe may be held against the foot to burn a mark where the shoe will sit. This causes the horse no pain but does create a lot of strong smelling smoke which may upset the horse. When the shoe is fitted to the foot it will be cooled in water. Some Farriers hot shoe on a regular basis as it is generally believed that a better fit can be obtained with a hot shoe.

THE HORSESHOE

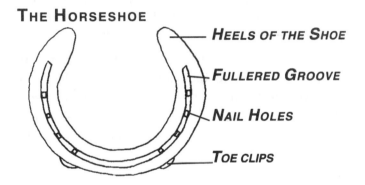

HEELS OF THE SHOE

FULLERED GROOVE

NAIL HOLES

TOE CLIPS

The heels of horse shoes may be "penciled" to reduce the risk of the hind foot catching the heel of the front shoe and levering the front shoe off. The fullered groove fills with dirt and gravel to act as an anti slipping device. The shoe itself can be made of concave metal which will help reduce suction, therefore decreasing the chance of the shoe being sucked off in deep going.

NAILING ON THE SHOE

When the shoe is fitted correctly it will be nailed to the foot. Nails come in different sizes and the Farrier will select the correct size for your horse and the shoe. The Farrier must apply the nails carefully so as not to penetrate the white line or other sensitive structures. The nails need to sit between the white line and the hoof wall. The ends of the nails appear on the outside of the hoof wall. Usually six to eight nails are used. The end of the nails are twisted off leaving a small end. This will become the clinch.

FINISHING THE FOOT

When all the nails are driven and the clinches prepared, the foot will be pulled forward and a small groove rasped under each clinch. All the clinches are tapped down or tightened with the clinching tongs. If clips are used these will be lightly tapped down into their place. To finish off, the rasp is used to smooth the clinches and run around the lower edge of the wall to minimize the risk of the hoof cracking.

THE NEWLY-SHOD FOOT

If your Farrier selection process was thorough, you will most likely be satisfied with the Farrier's work. There are certain things to look for in a newly shod foot. Most importantly look to see if the foot has retained its natural shape, and that the slope of the hoof matches the slope of the pastern and shoulder.

Check to see that the hoof wall has not been rasped away excessively. This will remove the protective covering of the hoof wall (the periople) and cause the hoof to dry and crack. In wet conditions and areas with abrasive footing the periople can be damaged by the environment. The Farrier will be able to recommend the correct course of action to help maintain the moisture level in the foot.

The hoof should have been trimmed to the correct length at both the toe and the heel. The inside and outside of the foot should be trimmed evenly, and the sole and frog may be lightly trimmed. In a healthy foot the frog should be in contact with the ground (obviously you will have to eyeball this!). Look to see if the clinches are all neatly in a line, are of a uniform shape and are smooth to the wall.

There should be no daylight between the shoe and the hoof, especially in the heel region. Whilst inspecting the heels, check the length of the heel of the shoe. The end of the shoe should not press on the soft heels of the foot, although a length of heel may extend beyond the end of the hoof. If a clip is used it should be neatly fitted and evenly shaped.

This is a lot to look for! With practice, your eye will become trained as to what a well shod foot looks like.

INDICATIONS THAT SHOEING IS NECESSARY

Even if your horse is on a regular shoeing schedule, be aware of any changes in the feet. If conditions change, for example the spring grass comes through suddenly, the hoof may grow more quickly than usual and require more frequent visits by the Farrier. Signs that the hoof needs attention include:

♦   Excessive growth of the hoof wall. The foot appears long and out of shape.

♦   A shoe is loose or lost.

♦   The shoes are worn thin, or an unshod horse is wearing his feet away faster then usual.

♦   The clinches have risen from the hoof wall.

♦   The hoof wall is cracking and crumbling around the nail line.

♦   The hoof wall is growing over the shoe.

FOOT PROBLEMS

The horse's foot can suffer from a number of conditions. Most of these can be avoided by paying attention to the hoof and providing correct care. Regular visits from your Farrier will go a long way towards ensuring the continued health of the horse's feet. The most common foot problems are:

BRUISES

The sole of the equine hoof can suffer from bruises caused by constant pounding, hard rocky surfaces, incorrect shoeing and poor conformation. These can be avoided by correct shoeing including the use of pads. People who live in areas that are stony often put leather or plastic pads on their horses to protect the soles. There are pros and cons with this which your Farrier can discuss with you.

Horses with flat feet are prone to bruising. This can be avoided by correct shoeing. A bruise appears as a red mark on the sole of the foot and is often discovered by the Farrier as he is preparing the hoof for shoeing. Bruises can cause irregular steps and indistinct lameness. Corns are bruises that occur at the seat of corn.

Treatment includes removing the cause and following the treatment procedures for abscesses.

ABSCESSES

CAUSES

These are caused by a foreign body penetrating the sensitive structures of the hoof. This can happen if the horse steps on a sharp object. Sometimes sand and grit can work their way into the foot causing an abscess (sometimes called a gravel.) Occasionally even the best Farrier will drive a nail too close to the white line and cause a pressure point, which if left unattended will turn into an abscess.

SYMPTOMS

After a visit from the Farrier check the temperature of the feet by placing the palm of your hand on the hoof wall. If one is warmer than the others it may indicate a suspect nail. Any "off" steps should not be ignored as they are a sure sign that something is amiss. Pick up the foot and lightly tap each nail head with a hammer. A reaction from the horse will indicate which nail is troublesome. Alternatively, wipe the nail line with a damp cloth and watch to see which area of the hoof dries the fastest. This is where the most heat is and probably the afflicted area.

Have the Farrier back to remove the offending nail and ask about follow up treatment. It may take several days after the Farriers visit for any symptoms to occur.

TREATMENT

Anytime a horse becomes suddenly lame, check his feet. This is the most likely site of lameness. The Vet can confirm your diagnosis and he or the Farrier can pare away the possible site in an attempt to relieve the internal pressure.

The usual treatment involves soaking the foot in Epsom salts and hot water (as hot as you can stand) to draw out the infection and pus in order to relieve the pressure. This is done at least twice a day for twenty minutes each. Between soakings pack the foot with poultice or Icthammol to draw out as much infection as possible. An Easy boot works well for this job, or you can create your own dressing with pieces of an empty feed sack and duct tape! Use the corner of the feed sack and strips of tape over the poultice to form a boot around the hoof. Be careful not to wrap the tape too tightly on or above the coronary band, because this may restrict circulation.

Relief will occur as soon as the pressure is relieved and the infection drained. This may be almost immediate or may take several days, depending on the severity of the initial wound or bruise.

THRUSH

CAUSES

This is a bacterial infection which can be caused by neglect. Standing in a wet and dirty stall will promote the bacteria which cause the disease. Some horses are built in such a way that they are prone to thrush no matter how well they are cared for.

SYMPTOMS

Bacteria thrive in warm, dark, damp conditions, and attack the cleft of the frog, producing a foul smelling substance that looks like crumbled white cheese. Some horses have such deep clefts that they are predisposed to thrush and these individuals must be carefully managed.

TREATMENT

Thrush which is treated promptly should not cause lameness, but feet that have suffered from severe neglect may develop other problems. Treatment consists of removing the cause. Keep the infected area clean and apply hydrogen peroxide directly to the cleft of the frog. This can be easily done with a syringe (without the needle).

Iodine can be used to clean out the cleft and in severe cases absorbent cotton can be packed into the cleft of the frog and then soaked with iodine. Your Farrier can assist in treating severe cases by paring away diseased tissue, and in extreme cases making special shoes.

Prevention consists of daily foot care and checking for signs of thrush. There are several products available that can be used as a preventative measure. Ask your Farrier if you need to use these or if your daily routine of cleaning the feet is sufficient. The stabled horse must have a clean and dry bed to stand on. A horse that lives outside needs a field which is dry to prevent a chronic thrush problem.

CRACKED HOOVES

CAUSES

Cracked hooves are caused by environmental conditions, excess stress and poor rasping. The feet will dry out if they are continually exposed to the wet. At certain times of the year this is virtually impossible to avoid. Cracks can also be caused by injury to the coronet band. When this happens the horn in that area will not grow properly,and a hole will appear at the coronet band. As the hoof grows down this split will grow down with it, creating cracks and splits as it reaches the ground surface.

SYMPTOMS

Splits and cracks appear on the hoof. They may start at the ground surface or from the coronet. Lameness is not usually present unless the crack is severe.

TREATMENT

For a bad crack the Farrier can provide suggestions that will help to stop the crack from progressing. If the crack is caused by environmental conditions (too wet or too dry), the Farrier will be able to advise you on the best course of action.

SEEDY TOE

CAUSES

Seedy toe is called separation when it occurs in other parts of the foot. This occurs when cavities form between the sensitive areas and the insensitive areas of the foot. The soft horn which holds the hoof together becomes diseased and disintegrates. Causes include dirt working up into the white line and bruising of the foot (most common in unshod horses.) Pressure from the clips of the shoe and direct injury to the wall can also cause the hoof to separate. Injury to the coronet band may damage the horn producing cells resulting in a separation as the foot grows downwards. Seedy toe may also be seen accompanying other problems such as laminitis.

SYMPTOMS

Frequently first noticed by the Farrier. As the foot is trimmed a hollow cavity filled with soft, broken down horn will be discovered. If left untreated this cavity will progress higher up the foot causing infection and lameness.

TREATMENT

If the cavity is not deep it can be pared away. Deeper holes may be packed with absorbent cotton soaked in iodine which will help to dry out the area and kill bacteria. Feed additives and the use of hoof products on the coronary band will help stimulate the growth of new horn.

LAMINITIS OR FOUNDER OF THE FEET

CAUSES

This is a horribly painful condition which can frequently be avoided by good management. Laminitis is caused by congestion of the vascular system within the hoof. As the name suggests it is an inflammation of the sensitive laminae.

Founder is caused by a disturbance of the vascular system. One of the most common causes is excessive feeding. Either breaking into the feed bin or gorging on rich grass. This type of laminitis is common in ponies as they often live out and over indulge!

Founder can also be caused by excessive work, especially in an unfit horse, and by placing excessive strain on one leg. This can occur if the horse is lame in one leg. By resting this leg he puts extra pressure on the other leg, causing that foot to founder.

Anything that upsets the vascular system can cause founder including stress and pregnancy.

SYMPTOMS

A horse suffering from laminitis is a sorry sight. Usually there is a lack of willingness to move. The classic stance of a foundering horse is the front feet out in front of the horse with the majority of the weight resting on the heels. The hind feet are up under the body bearing as much of the weight as possible. The horse may lay down a lot to try to relieve the pain in his feet.

The feet are usually hot with a pounding pulse. Respiration will be increased and the horse will appear depressed and uneasy. In extreme cases the pedal bone will rotate causing pressure on the sole and even penetrating the sole.

TREATMENT

Veterinary advise should be sought immediately. If the patient is a pony suffering from too much grass remove him from the cause of his pain. Effective treatment involves soaking the feet to reduce congestion and pressure. The Vet will prescribe drugs to help with the pain and reduce the pressure in the foot.

The Farrier will be able to help with special shoes and will need to work with the Vet to find the best treatment. The most useful thing an owner can do is to prevent founder. In most cases it is avoidable and in a well organized stable should not be a problem. Keep a close eye on ponies and restrict their intake if necessary. A pony with a large firm crest is a prime candidate for laminitis. This pony will need a strict diet and lots of exercise.

NAVICULAR SYNDROME

The navicular bone is a small shuttle shaped bone located at the rear of the foot. The deep flexor tendon glides over the navicular bone. In navicular syndrome the bone becomes pitted and develops rough edges. This roughening of the bone causes irritation and pain to the tendons and thus lameness. In certain cases inflammation of the bursa around the joint sheath will cause the pain.

CAUSES

Navicular generally occurs in older horses although it can be found in a young horse. Pounding and excessive work can cause navicular. A careless Farrier who does not pay attention to the angle of the feet could over time create stress on the deep flexor tendon and navicular bone. Low heels, small feet and upright pasterns may predispose a horse to navicular syndrone.

SYMPTOMS

Unexplained lameness can often be attributed to navicular. Sometimes the horse will be sound and sometimes not, especially the day after strenuous work. In the early stages rest is sufficient to relieve the pain. The lameness may appear to shift from one foot to the other depending on which is under most stress. For example, in a turn the inside foreleg will appear to be more painful. Navicular almost always affects both front feet.

As the problem worsens the horse will be uneasy on his feet and will "point" (stand with one foot ahead of the other) one or both front feet. Lameness will be more pronounced going down hill and on rough ground.

As the disease progresses the horse will develop a shuffling gait, the strides will be shortened and he will attempt to put the toe down first. Over time the hoof will become more boxy in appearance. If navicular is suspected a confirmation of the diagnosis may be made with X-rays. These will also indicate the degree of damage. In cases where there is a question as to the cause of lameness the Vet will perform a nerve block. This temporarily numbs all the nerves to the heel region. If this is where the pain is the horse will now be sound. Incidentally, if there is a lesser lameness in the other foot it will show up now.

It is worth mentioning that there are horses with X-rays indicating advanced navicular that have never suffered from lameness and also horses with perfect X-rays that have symptoms of the disease. Recent studies have shown that each case should be individually evaluated and all circumstances considered.

TREATMENT

Navicular disease is not curable however, there are ways of managing the syndrome which, especially if started early enough, will prolong the useful life of the horse. Your Vet and Farrier can work together to develop a plan. Corrective trimming and shoeing together with medication can very often control the problem for a period.

In extreme cases the horse can be denerved. This deprives the foot of sensation and so the horse will go sound. Care must be taken to check for other injuries which the horse will not feel or react to. In some cases the nerves may grow back causing more pain. Many horses have benefited from denerving but all aspects must be carefully considered. A denerved horse cannot be sold as sound.

NO FOOT NO HORSE!

The horse's feet are essential to his well being and usefulness. The horse owner can help considerably with the continued health of the horse's feet by being familiar with the norm. Scheduling regular visits with the Farrier will aid in the early detection of problems. The single most important task for the horse owner is to monitor the feet, and observe any changes in appearance or gait.

The detail included in this chapter is not intended to alarm the reader, but it is intended to educate the reader as to the possible problems horses can encounter. Being aware of potential problems, will help the horse owner avoid serious medical conditions.

INTERNAL STRUCTURE OF THE FOOT

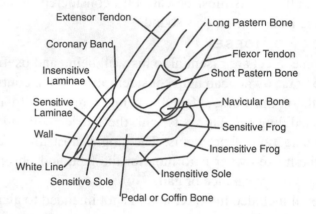

AFTERWORD

Horse ownership is something that many people dream about. Yes, it is financially expensive however, the rewards are worth more than money. A horse of your own can be your special friend, an impartial confidant and a source of great personal satisfaction. There is nothing more satisfying than watching your horse playing in the paddock, seeing his well toned muscles rippling underneath his shiny coat and knowing the reason he looks and feels so good is thanks to your care.

Finding a horse that suits your needs can be a long and sometimes frustrating experience. Please take your time when you are horse hunting. In the long run it will save you time, money and heartache. There are plenty of good horses out there and horse shopping should be a fun, learning experience.

Taking care of your own horse basically comes down to being observant. Knowing what is normal and what is not. Study your horse's habits, it is surprising how many people miss out on their horse's personality.

I hope you will use this book as a reference for all your horse care problems. Let me know if you have any horse care secrets that could be included in future editions. I am always keen to hear about peoples horse experiences, good and bad! Comments and suggestions for future improvements are welcomed and encouraged.

Happy horsekeeping!

Jacqueline Dwelle

Jacqueline Dwelle

Appendix

EQUINE SUPPLY CATALOGS

These are often a source of veterinary supplies including wormers, wound dressings and other medical supplies. Frequently these suppliers stock other equestrian products which can be cheaper than they would be locally.

American Livestock Supply
P.O. Box 8441
Madison, WI 53708-8441
1-800-356-0700

Big D's Tack and Vet Supply
P.O. Box 247
Northfield, OH 44067
1-800-321-2142

Horse Health USA
P.O. Box 9101
Canton, OH 44711-9101
1-800-321-0235

KV Vet Supply
P.O. Box 245
David City, NE 68632
402-367-6047

United Vet Equine
14101 West 62nd Street
Eden Prairie, MN 55346
1-800-328-6652

Valley Vet Supply
P.O. Box 504
Marysville, KS 66508-0504
1-800-356-1005

Wiese Vet Supply
P.O. Box 1308
Atkinson, NH 03811-1308
1-800-869-4373

Jeffers Equine
PO Box 100
Dothan, AL 36302 -0100
1-800-533- 3377

American Farrier's Association
4059 Iron Works Pike
Lexington, KY 40511
606-233-7411
Fax 606-231-7862

American Association of Equine Practitioners
4075 Iron Works Pike
Lexington, KY 40511
606-233-0147
800-443-0177

Glossary

AAEP American Association of Equine Practitioners.

AFA American Farriers Association.

Alfalfa A legume grass used to make hay.

Anthelmintics The family of drugs used to control parasites in horses.

Anti-sweat sheet A light sheet designed to dry or cool a wet or hot horse.

Anticast roller A body surcingle with a metal loop over the withers to prevent the horse from rolling over and being cast against the wall.

Ascarids Also known as round worms, ascarids are an internal parasite.

Automatic water A device that automatically refills with water as the horse drinks.

Bandage pad A large square pad, often quilted, which is applied underneath a bandage or wrap.

Bandages Also called wraps. Provide support, warmth and protection.

Boarding stable A stable that provides boarding services for horses, may offer a variety of services.

Boarding Contract A contract between a boarding stable and an owner, stipulating responsibility, services to be provided and other details.

Body brush A soft brush, often with a handle, used for grooming the head, body and legs.

Bot fly Similar to a bee in appearance, the bot fly lays eggs on the horse. These are licked off and the larvae complete their life cycle inside the horse.

Bottom Line Lower profile of the horse running from the throat, between the front legs to the sheath.

Bow Describes the shape of a strained tendon. Often used in reference to an old injury.

Broken wind A horse is said to have broken wind when his breathing is labored due to damage of his lungs.

Broken down Another term for a sprained tendon.

Brushing When one hoof strikes the other leg as the horse moves.

Bucket Insulator A plastic device which holds a bucket, preventing the water from freezing in cold weather.

Buffer The tool used by the Farrier to raise the clinches before removing the shoe.

Bursa The fluid filled sac around joints. Its purpose is to lubricate the joint.

Capped hock A bursal enlargement occurring on the point of the hock.

Capped elbow A bursal enlargement occurring on the elbow joint. Also called a shoe boil.

Capped Knee A bursal enlargement occurring on the knee.

Cast A horse is said to be cast when he is unable to get up.

Cleft of frog The groove running down the center of the frog.

Clinch The turned over end of a horse shoe nail. The clinches hold the shoe in place.

Clinching tongs Tool used to tighten the clinches.

Clipping Removal of hair during the winter to make care and work easier.

Coggins test A blood test for Equine Infectious Anemia.

Cold Therapy The use of cold to help reduce pain and swelling.

Colic Any sort of abdominal pain.

Concave shoe Reduces the risk of loosing a shoe due to suction in deep going.

Conformation How a horse is built.

Conformation faults Any deviation from the norm. See table starting page 43.

Contracted Heels Heels that are narrow and upright. Contracted heels place pressure on the rest of the hoof.

Cooling out The process of bringing the horses temperature, pulse and respiration to a resting rate following exercise.

COPD Chronic Obstructive Pulmonary Disease. Another name for broken wind or heaves.

Corns Bruises which occur at the seat of corn. Characterized by a red mark often found by the Farrier.

Coupling Space between the last rib and the point of hip.

Cresty An over developed crest. Associated with horses that are close to foundering and stallions.

Cribbing A vice. The horse grabs a solid object between his teeth, arches his neck and sucks in wind. As he does this he makes a sound similar to a burp.

Crimping A method of processing oats and other grains to make them more digestible.

Cross-ties A pair of chains or other material attached to the wall at one end and the horse's halter at the other. Designed to restrain the horse during grooming or other procedures.

Curb Caused by strain to the ligament below the hock. Appears as a swelling below the point of hock.

Curry comb May be made out of rubber, plastic or metal. The rubber and plastic curry combs are used to groom the horse, the metal varieties are used to clean the other brushes.

Dandy brush A stiff brush for removing heavy dirt and when dampened for laying the mane over.

Denerve To cut the nerves leading to the hoof, in order to remove pain and feeling.

Deworming Administration of worm medicine for the purpose of parasite control. A regular procedure.

Double fence Building separate fences for each paddock. Usually 12 feet between paddocks.

Drawing knife Knife used by the Farrier to trim the hoof.

Easy boot Used as a temporary replacement for a lost shoe. Made of rubber with metal fittings.

Electrolytes A feed supplement which provides essential salts. Usually only fed to horses in hard work or hot climates.

Equine Infectious Anemia Contagious disease with no cure. Tested for with the coggins test.

Ergot Growth of horn found at the back of the fetlock.

Ewe Neck Neck with more muscle on the underside than the top. Appears to be upside-down.

Extruded Feed Feed product produced by heat and pressure. Contains a mixture of basic grains and other ingredients.

Fecal exam Microscopic examination of fecal matter to detect parasite load.

Fight of flight The horses natural instinct, left over from the times when horses were hunted animals.

Flexion test Performed by the Vet to test for weakness in the joints of the legs.

Floating Process of filing the rough edges off of the teeth.

Forge Furnace used by the Farrier to heat horse shoes during the process of fitting the shoes.

Forging The sound heard when the hind shoe strikes the underside of the front shoe.

Founder Inflammation of the sensitive laminae, causing intense pain within the feet.

Frog Triangular shaped growth of soft horn located on the sole of the foot. Acts as a shock absorber, anti-slip device and as a pump to push the blood back up the leg.

Fullered groove The groove in the horse shoe which fills with dirt to help reduce slipping.

Furacin Anti-septic ointment.

Grab Wound caused when the hind foot strikes the back of the foreleg, usually in the heel region.

Grass hay Hay made with grasses such as timothy, rye grass and orchard grass.

Hard feed Another name for grains and other bagged horse feeds.

Harrow Also called a drag. Dragged behind a tractor it is used to spread manure and prevent holes from forming.

Heart rate At rest 36-42 beats per minute.

Heat therapy The use of heat to draw infection out of wounds and in some cases to reduce pain. Can be alternated with cold therapy.

Heaves Another name for broken wind.

Hives Lumps or bumps that appear on any part of the body.

Hoof dressing Applied to the hooves to enhance appearance and as a hoof conditioner.

Hoof testers Used by the Vet or Farrier to search for sore spots in the hoof.

Hoof pick Used to clean dirt out of the feet.

Hot fomentations Method of applying heat therapy, using hot water and towels.

Hot wired To electrify a portion of fence using a battery designed for this purpose..

Ichthammol Anti-septic ointment which also acts as a drawing agent.

Impaction Partial or complete blockage in the bowel or intestines.

Interfering General term used for a hoof striking any of the other legs or feet.

Kicking A vice, initially triggered by an outside stimuli. Can become a habit.

Laminae The structure which links the sensitive and insensitive areas of the hoof. The sensitive and insensitive laminae interlock.

Laminitis Inflammation of the laminae, also called founder.

Laser therapy The use of cold lasers to treat wounds and other injuries.

Legumes Variety of grasses used to make hay. Usually high in protein, includes alfalfa and red clover.

Lucerne Another name for alfalfa.

Lyme disease Debilitating disease spread by ticks.

Magnetic therapy Use of magnetic blankets or boots to expedite the healing of soft tissue.

Meadow hay Hay made from permanent pasture

Microbial Fermentation Digestive process which makes use of bacteria to breakdown food.

Mud Fever Skin condition where the hair on the legs falls out due to wet conditions.

Navicular bone Shuttle shaped bone located at the rear of the hoof behind the pedal bone.

Navicular syndrome Irritation to the tendons running over the navicular bone or inflammation of the bursa in that region.

Nerve block Medical procedure done to test for pain in one of the feet.

Over tracking When the hind foot lands in front of the track left by the front foot.

Over-reach Another name for a grab.

Pellets A form of processed feed

Periople Thin coating on the hoof wall, like varnish. Its purpose is to retain moisture.

Pincers Tool used by Farrier to remove the shoe.

Pinworms An internal parasite.

Pointing Standing with one fore foot in advance of the other for an extended period. May indicate pain.

Poultice Medicinal mud used to draw heat and swelling out of a bruised or strained area.

Pre Purchase Exam Examination performed by a Vet prior to purchasing a horse.

Psyllium The fiber found in products designed to rid the digestive tract of sand.

Puncture Wound A wound which is deeper than its entrance.

Quartering Traditionally, this was a brief grooming that was done before exercise. Following exercise the horse was thoroughly groomed, or strapped. Not practiced much any more.

Radiographs X-rays

Rain rot or scald Skin condition associated with damp conditions and hair loss.

Rasp Tool used by Farrier to file the hoof .

Rectal exam Physical exam performed by a Vet.

Respiratory rate At rest 8-15 breaths per minute.

Ringbone Bony enlargement on the pastern.

Roller Used to secure blankets. Usually padded at the withers.

Rolling Done to make grains more palatable and digestible.

Round pen Small circular paddock used for breaking and training.

Scratches Wounds in the heel area caused by excess moisture.

Scrim Light weight sheet used for drying and cooling.

Seed hay Hay made from grass grown specifically for this purpose. May be first, second or third cutting.

Seedy Toe Condition resulting from the separation of the hoof at the white line.

Shoe boil Also called capped elbow.

Short of a rib A horse that is long coupled is said to be "short of a rib."

Short feed Also called hard feed or grain.

Side bone A bony enlargement which appears on the pastern.

Smegma Black, greasy substance produced in the sheath area of male horses. May accumulate and cause problems with urination. Periodic cleaning of the sheath removes excess smegma.

Sore shins Inflammation which appears on the cannon bone caused by hard work.

Spavin Swelling either hard or soft occurring in the hock region.

Splint Bony enlargement which forms on the splint or cannon bones.

Steaming Method of processing grains to increase digestibility.

Strongyles Also called blood worms. These are an internal parasite.

Supplements Products fed in addition to the traditional grains and hay. Often specifically designed to aid a particular problem.

Sweat Procedure used to break up a long standing lump or area of filling.

Sweat scraper Tool used to scrape excess water or sweat from the coat.

Synovial fluid Fluid which lubricates the joints. Contained inside the bursal sac.

Synovial membrane Produces synovial fluid.

Temperature At rest 99 °F- 101°F (38°C)

Textured feed A mixed horse feed frequently called sweet feed.

Thoroughpin Bursal enlargement located on each side of the hock.

Thrush Bacterial foot disease, often caused by neglect, resulting in a strong smelling, white, crumbly discharge.

Toe clip Area of the shoe raised and wrapped over the wall to hold the shoe in place.

Toeing knife Also called a drawing or hoof knife.

Top Line Line running from the poll to the top of the tail.

Trace clip Style of clip where the belly and underside of the neck only are removed.

Tram lines Lines left after clipping.

Turn-out blanket Blanket designed to be worn in the paddock. Come in many styles, one of the popular types is called a New Zealand blanket.

Twisted gut A portion of intestine that flips over on itself causing intense pain and colic.

Ultra-sound Technique used to study tendon damage. Same technology that is used on pregnant women (and mares!)

Undercutting When the toe of the fore foot scrapes the toe of the hind foot as it is lifted.

Warbles A fly which lays its eggs on the horse. These eggs become larvae and these become internal parasites.

Warming up Process of slowly warming the horses muscles with easy work before asking for strenuous activity.

Weaving A vice in which the horse sways from side to side. Considered an unsoundness.

White line The area of the hoof where the sensitive and insensitive laminae join.

Wind sucking Similar to cribbing. A wind sucker does not need a solid object on which to rest his teeth.

Windpuff or windgall A bursal enlargement occurring in the fetlock region.

Worming Same as deworming.

Index

Order Form

ORDER A COPY FOR A FRIEND!

Please send me the following books:

_____

_____

_____

I understand that I may return the books for a full refund-for any reason.

NAME:

ADDRESS:

CITY:

STATE:

ZIP:

PHONE:

Please add 6% for books shipped to North Carolina addresses. Shipping $4.00 for first book and $2.00 for each additional book.

Total:_____

SEND YOUR ORDER TO:
Hoofbeat Publications
30080 Deercroft Drive
Wagram, NC 28396

PEOPLE WHO GENUINELY CARE ABOUT HORSES!

Visit Our Web Site!

Hoofbeat Publications maintains a dynamic web site. As new publications are developed and made ready for our customers, we add excerpts and diagrams to the web site.

Currently our web pages contain extracts from the pre publication draft of *Your First Horse*. These excerpts are available for anyone to review. By the time you read this there will be more accurate horse care information on our pages for you to read at your leisure! Watch our web site for new books and reports.

Hoofbeat Publications is run by dedicated horse people and is genuinely concerned about the welfare of all our equine friends. It is with this in mind that we ask for your comments, criticisms and suggestions. If there is a horse care issue that you would like to see included in future publications please let us know. We are asking for your help with future publications, so that we can provide you with the information that you need!

Hoofbeat Publications can be found at:
http://www.firsthorse.com
or send us Email at:
jackie@firsthorse.com

PEOPLE WHO GENUINELY CARE ABOUT HORSES!